SUSTAINABLE MINISTRY

SUSTAINABLE MINISTRY

How to Lead (and When to Nap)

MARGARET J. MARCUSON

AN ALBAN BOOK

t&tclark

LONDON · NEW YORK · OXFORD · NEW DELHI · SYDNEY

T&T CLARK

Bloomsbury Publishing Inc, 1359 Broadway, New York, NY 10018, USA
Bloomsbury Publishing Plc, 50 Bedford Square, London, WC1B 3DP, UK
Bloomsbury Publishing Ireland, 29 Earlsfort Terrace, Dublin 2, D02 AY28, Ireland

BLOOMSBURY, T&T CLARK and the T&T Clark logo are trademarks of
Bloomsbury Publishing Plc

First published in the United States of America 2026

For legal purposes the Acknowledgments on p. viii constitute an extension of this
copyright page.

Cover design: Diana Nuhn

Cover image © iStock.com/ekolara

Cover design by Enterline Design Services

Scripture quotations are from New Revised Standard Version Bible, copyright ©
1989 National Council of the Churches of Christ in the United States of America.
Used by permission. All rights reserved worldwide.

Bloomsbury Publishing Inc does not have any control over, or responsibility for,
any third-party websites referred to or in this book. All internet addresses given
in this book were correct at the time of going to press. The author and publisher
regret any inconvenience caused if addresses have changed or sites have ceased
to exist, but can accept no responsibility for any such changes.

Library of Congress Cataloging-in-Publication Data

available at http://lccn.loc.gov/2015040044

ISBN: HB: 979-8-2163-7804-4
PB: 979-8-2163-7800-6
ePDF: 979-8-2163-7802-0
eBook: 979-8-2163-7801-3

Typeset by Deanta Global Publishing Services, Chennai, India
Printed and bound in the United States of America

For product safety related questions contact productsafety@bloomsbury.com.

To find out more about our authors and books visit www.bloomsbury.com and
sign up for our newsletters.

To Karl, for everything.
Thank you for your support, patience, and for being my
biggest fan.

CONTENTS

Acknowledgments viii

1 Introduction: Are You Exhausted? 1

2 Get Clear: What Is Your Work? 7

3 Get Connected: Who Do You Need to Relate To? 21

4 Get Reflective: Who Are You? 37

5 Get to the Money: What Is Your Role? 57

6 Communication: Can You Get Free of
Needing People to Agree? 77

7 Get Focused: What Do You Want to Do Most? 101

8 Get Prayerful: What Matters in Ministry? 123

Note to the Reader 139
Appendix A: Sustain Yourself in Ministry: An Inventory 140
Appendix B: "What Do You Want" Planning Guide 143
Appendix C: Staff Planning Questionnaire 151
Appendix D: Money/Stewardship Tips 153
Recommended Resources 155
Notes 158
About the Author 164

ACKNOWLEDGMENTS

"Since we are surrounded by so great a cloud of witnesses . . . ." (Heb. 12:1, NRSV) I am surrounded by so great a cloud of readers. I'm grateful to every single one.

Thank you to teacher and editor extraordinaire Katie Long. Her "Essentials of Writing Based in Bowen Theory" seminar jump-started this book. Katie gave thoughtful initial feedback. She did a preliminary edit of all but one chapter. Jill Kelly, my first writing coach, edited the "Leaders Who Last" modules, the genesis of this book. Richard Brown, my editor at Bloomsbury, was a champion of the book from the beginning.

Thank you to colleagues who gave feedback on chapters: Courtney Rice Alford, Liz Leavitt, Jabulani McCalister, Luke Maybry, Laurie Newman, Scott Painter, John Schraan, and Mindi Welton-Mitchell. Marianne LaBarre and Skip Johnson read the book before this book (the one that didn't quite work . . .).

Thank you to: Israel Galindo for his clear thinking, and for coordinating the Leadership in Ministry workshop. All my LIM colleagues, especially Meg Hess, Rebecca Maccini, and Elaine Boomer for 25 years in the Boston workshop. Jake Morrill for our meaningful work in Leading with Depth and for all the fun. And to Cindy Maybeck for helping me think more clearly about my work and my life.

My own immediate and extended family increased my capacity for life. I continue to learn from my husband, Karl, and our wonderful young adult children, Hannah and Hugh. Their encouragement helped keep me going on this book.

Finally, thank you to all my clergy clients over the past 25 years. You taught me about your unique context for life in ministry. Your commitment and persistence inspire me.

1

Introduction
Are You Exhausted?

Come to me, all you that are weary and are carrying heavy burdens, and I will give you rest. Take my yoke upon you, and learn from me; for I am gentle and humble in heart, and you will find rest for your souls. For my yoke is easy, and my burden is light.

—MATT. 11:28-30 (NRSV)

Rest

Rest for your souls. That's what most church leaders I know need. It's been a long journey, and everyone is exhausted. Who hasn't been carrying heavy burdens?

My husband, Karl, loves a genre of YouTube videos in which one comedian plays all the parts. In one of these, Julie Nolke plays both herself and her roommate arguing about grammar.[1] In another, Ryan George puts on a variety of facial hair to represent different people creating the teddy bear.[2] These videos remind me of the multiple roles that have been forced on clergy over these past years. They've had to be not just preacher and provider of pastoral care but also play roles from tech expert to video presenter to hybrid program developer—not to mention leading through an unknown wilderness. For years. No wonder you're tired.

How do you find rest for your soul—not just a day off, vacation, or even sabbatical—but a soul-deep rest? In Becky Chambers's book *A Prayer for the Crown Shy*, a character thinks, "They'd spent too much time around tired folks to not recognize the same condition in themself [*sic*]. They were running up against a wall, and it didn't matter whether they understood where the wall had come from, or what it was made of. The only way to get through it was to stop trying, for a while."[3] How do you stop trying, for a while?

I do notice clergy have a hard time showing grace to themselves. The most responsible and hard-working clergy are the ones who are hardest on themselves. If you are reading this book, you may be one of them. They are the least likely to give themselves a break or allow others to share the load. In the throes of lockdown, one pastor told me he was trying to extend "covid grace" to himself. If he wanted to work in his pajamas, he didn't beat himself up for not feeling like getting dressed. He just got busy with work right in his pajamas. Grace still abounds in these post-COVID years. I pray that as a preacher of the gospel message you can take the gospel words of grace and hope into yourselves.

Discern the Work

Sabbath rest was not seven days a week. It was one out of six. There was, and is, work to do. You have sermons to prepare, hybrid worship to plan, hospital visits to make, staff (also exhausted) to supervise, and budgets to review. However, there are some ways to make the "yoke" a little easier. Working less may be part of it, but it's also about having a different relationship with the work. To do the right work for right now, because it's your work to do, not what someone else thinks you should do.

Jeremiah 6:16 says, "Thus says the Lord: Stand at the crossroads, and look, and ask for the ancient paths, where the good way lies; and walk in it, and find rest for your souls" (NRSV).[4] Where does the good way lie now? It will require not just doing. You will also need to pause, looking back, around, and ahead to discern where you think the good way lies, at least the way to get started on. One pastor said he was working to develop a "flashlight purpose," just enough clarity to get going toward the light he has discerned. He didn't know what the future would bring, but he could get enough clarity to get started.

Carl Jung suggested people "quietly do the next and most necessary thing."[5] I wonder what that would be like in our much more pressured and noisier world. Could you do the next and most necessary thing, without feeling the burden of the future or even of the present? In this moment, what is God calling you to do? It might be to check email or texts. It might be to call your favorite church member, the one who always lifts you up. It might be to prayerfully read the text for Sunday. It might be (really!) a nap. Even the nap might be the "practice of the presence," as Brother Lawrence said.[6]

Walking in "the good way" means making a decision and taking the risk to step onto that path. In this uncertain time, it will not be a smooth way even if it's a good way. The disciples may have looked back as they faced opposition and persecution and thought, "What easy yoke?! What was that about, Jesus?" There is hard work ahead. But it's not yours alone.

Share the Load

Ministry is not a one-person show. You don't discern the future and step onto the path ahead alone. Relationships with others are essential, and the work of the church is shared. Sometimes you carry not just your burden but other people's as well. That adds up to an even heavier load. "Come to Jesus, all you that are weary and carrying heavy burdens—including the ones that may not belong to you."

I talked with a pastor recently who faced a year of challenges in recruiting lay leadership for the coming year. The usual suspects had done their time. There wasn't a queue of prospective leaders as there had been in the past. She recognized this was not just a short-term problem. It required longer term thinking for the years ahead. She tossed and turned about it until she realized this wasn't hers to carry alone. This was not her problem, but the church's problem. She shared the challenge with lay leaders, and ultimately with the congregation. They were able to think together about how to manage leadership needs in the future in new ways. It was a relief to her to set down the extra responsibility and allow others to carry it.

Ministry is never going to be easy. And in these times when no one knows what the future holds, it is harder than ever. It's been said that these words for Matthew are "not an invitation to a life of ease, but of deliverance from the artificial burdens of human religion."[7] I wonder what deliverance from the artificial burdens of pastoral ministry would look like, especially the burden of thinking it's all up to you. The load of ministry is easier to carry when you take on what is yours to do. And let others carry what belongs to them. The work of discernment means discovering what the call is right now, for you, and for your community. Then setting forth on the path to do the work *together*, little by little.

In my own life in ministry, in a far less anxious time in the church and in the world, I hit a wall. In an ordinary smallish church with no more than the ordinary problems of ministry, I didn't know if I could go on. By the grace of God, I encountered the work of Rabbi Edwin Friedman, his book *Generation to Generation*, and his training program for clergy. Through Friedman, I learned about Murray Bowen and his family systems theory.

This book is anchored in the work of Murray Bowen. Bowen was one of the founders of the family therapy movement. He developed a comprehensive theory of how people relate to one another in their families, and how those patterns and processes are passed down through the family's generations and in other groups and organizations. Why use a secular theory to talk about church leadership? Bowen's ideas accurately describe how relationship processes work. They provide a map for navigating difficulties and making the most of people's strengths. Bowen theory is in no way a substitute for Scripture, theology, or spirituality. However, it can be a practical and useful complement to them and a valuable tool for leaders. It was transformative for me. I learned to discern where my real responsibilities lay. I began to be more responsible for myself and how I related to others, and to worry less about other people and what they did and didn't do. It was a big relief. This new perspective enabled me to continue in ministry, first in the local church, and then as a support to other parish pastors.

In this book, we'll look at ways for you to:

- Get Clear on what your work is—and what it is not.

- Get Connected with others in ways that are life-giving for you and for them.

- Get Reflective about yourself: who you are and how you want to grow.

- Get to the Money: handle ministry funding in uncertain times.

- Get Free of Needing People to Agree: improve your communication (outgoing *and* incoming).

- Get Focused on what you want to do most.

- Get Prayerful, so you can remember what matters in ministry.

I recommend you read this book a chapter at a time. Beginning with Chapter 2, I provide questions for reflections. Stop and reflect on one or two of the questions. Then another day, take on the next chapter. The book has a sequence, but if one chapter jumps out at you, start there.

Finally, let's remember and use the prayer of St. Teresa of Avila. I like to say these words of hers every day: "Let nothing disturb you, nothing frighten you. All things are passing, God never changes! Patient endurance attains to all things. Who God possesses in nothing is wanting, alone God suffices."[8]

2

Get Clear

What Is Your Work?

Let the favor of the Lord our God be upon us, and prosper for us the work of our hands—O prosper the work of our hands!
—PSALM 90:17 (NRSV)

My first job out of seminary was as interim pastor of the First Spanish-American Baptist Church in San Jose, California. This was long before the idea of trained interims came along. They needed an interim who knew Spanish. I spoke some Spanish, and the denomination matched us up. I remember walking the halls of that little church, age 26, thinking and praying, "God, I have no idea how to do this job." Quite apart from the language challenges, I felt at sea in handling the nuts and bolts of pastoral ministry. Every seminary grad knows they don't teach you everything you need to know.

When my initial three-month contract was about to end, I was shocked to discover in an all-church meeting that they were considering not renewing it. I was able to speak up for myself—not my greatest strength back then—and they did extend my contract. Of course, I was right, and they were right: I really didn't know how to do the job. But I learned fast after that crisis and completed a full year as their interim. (And my Spanish was a lot better by then.) Better late than never, I learned the way into that community. I focused first on improving worship and preaching, even in imperfect Spanish. Second, I worked to connect with folks, especially through pastoral care. I made a lot of mistakes. Yet once I got clear that my job wasn't to make them like me but to be a pastoral presence for them, everything went a lot better.

There are endless opportunities to get clearer in ministry. In later chapters I'll address clarity about who you are, how you want to relate to others, and how you spend your time. In this chapter we'll begin with two key things to clarify: (1) what your work is, and (2) what your work isn't. The second is as important as the first, perhaps even more important.

First, get clear about what your work is. Ministry involves real, hard work. You already know you can't get away from that, especially now. Most clergy have a job quite different from what they had at the beginning of 2020. Years later, everything is much more fluid and uncertain and difficult. That's all the more reason to increase clarity about what your work is.

Give Them the Bigger Picture

The work of pastoral leadership is, first of all, to frame reality for people and help them find ways to learn and grow spiritually in response to that reality. This doesn't mean you tell them what to think or how to be. Rather, you provide a bigger context for what is going on in their lives, in the church and in the world.

At the beginning of the pandemic shutdown, one pastor told his congregation, "We don't know everything that is happening right now, but here is what we will be doing: we will have worship each week in some way. We will continue to be a community who supports one another. We will continue our prayerful presence with each other and with our world." At a time of great anxiety, he offered them a framework for their life together even though they couldn't gather in person.

For senior pastoral leaders, your role includes framing the ministry context and hopes for the future. Don't panic—you don't have to know it all or do it all. Even in the short term, when you have a clear sense of direction, it lowers people's anxiety. They have a sense that someone is in charge, and it calms them down.

You may say, "I'm not a visionary. Not only that, I'm too exhausted to even think about the future. I'm just trying to get by week to week." But you don't have to know everything. You simply need to be able to think a little bigger than those around you. No one else has your position; no one else can see what you see. However, you don't have to chart a course in isolation. The future, even for the short term, is developed in conversation with other key leaders.

How can you do this, when no one knows what is going to happen in church or in the wider world? In these uncertain times, you may be able to say something like this: "Here's what I see for the near term. While none of us knows what's going to happen in the future, here are my own highest priorities right now." You don't dictate a plan. Rather, you offer a big-picture perspective to begin a conversation with key lay and staff leaders.[1]

Even a one-year plan must be adaptable nowadays. There's nothing wrong with that. It's being in touch with reality. I've been working with pastors on developing a simple 90-day plan, and that's what I do for myself. A short-term framework helps people be a little calmer and more energized. One pastor said, "My anxious wiring overloads and gets lost gazing over the whole map rather than just watching for the next mile marker."

Take the time to think through where you're going right now and what your own principles and immediate purpose are. Then you will have a framework for decision-making and the scope of the work moving forward. Clear priorities are in place for your work: "I'm focusing on this, and not this, for now."

This leads to an ongoing process of trying something, assessing its effectiveness, and adapting. The consulting world calls this "action research." It's on-the-ground experimentation and adjustment. Now more than ever, plans are not fixed in stone. Overseeing such a process is part of your work.

If you have a secondary leadership role, you can do this work within your area of responsibility. Think through where you are heading in the short term, no more than one year, probably less, in the context of the wider mission of the church. This makes a huge contribution to ministry, now and into the future.

One associate pastor in a Lutheran church struggled to get the youth program going after in-person events started again. He knew he wanted to integrate the youth more fully into the church's life, with strong intergenerational connections. The church had historically had a strong youth group. People expected that a traditional youth group would restart just as it had been before. He worked to clarify his own values and beliefs, and how to apply them in this context. He had to think short-term. Each quarter he assessed how youth, parents, and the rest of the congregation, including the senior minister, were responding to his efforts.

What if you are new to a church? It takes time to be part of the congregation. When you begin, you aren't part of the system. You don't understand the territory well enough to know what might make sense for them. Your purpose is to get connected, to develop relationships. Yet from the beginning, you can exercise leadership as you deepen your own thinking about your ministry principles. You can begin to understand how to apply them in *this* context. You can share with people your principles and your first thoughts on priorities as you get to know the congregation.

Attend to the Nuts and Bolts

Second, in addition to framing the bigger picture, your work is to see that things get done. This is the work of *administration.* Don't groan! Administration is not doing it all yourself. That's the path to exhaustion and burnout.

Administration is part of all church leadership roles. Israel Galindo says: ". . . inspiration without perspiration tends to get you nowhere. People may stand and applaud a vision, but concrete goals will get them to roll up their sleeves and get to purposeful work."[2]

There's a big difference between getting things done and *seeing* that things get done. Engaging others in the work of ministry helps you with the work. Giving them a chance to use their gifts is a gift to *them,* as they become engaged in what Galindo calls purposeful work.

How you do this in practice will vary depending on your denomination, the size of the church, and the size of your staff. One pastor of a small Baptist church asked the chair of the worship committee to recruit Sunday morning Scripture readers. The two of them together developed some guidelines for readers. The pastor had been asking the same people over and over. He discovered the worship chair had a different circle. New people, including some children and youth, began participating in worship leadership. And the pastor had one less thing to do for worship preparation each week.

The pastor of a multi-staff Presbyterian church took on additional responsibility during a time of staff transition. She stepped in during the staffing gap and continued as two new staff members got up to speed. Her operations manager pointed out to her that she was holding on to responsibilities. The pastor realized she was keeping the new staff from learning and claiming their roles. Not only was she working far too hard, she was getting in the way of her new team. She then was able to step back and focus on the important work that really was hers to do. That gave the team the chance to use their gifts in the work they were hired to do.

Remember, as Paul says, "We have gifts that differ according to the grace given to us: prophecy, in proportion to faith; ministry, in ministering; the teacher, in teaching; the exhorter, in exhortation; the giver, in generosity; the leader, in diligence; the compassionate, in cheerfulness" (Rom. 12:6-8, NRSV). Wise leaders have the humility to recognize where they need help, and the discernment to recognize where others are gifted.

Practically, when you carry too many of the administrative details on your shoulders, you do a disservice to the church. If it all depends on you, when you leave, it can all fall apart. When you develop the gifts of others and create structures for getting things done, you give a gift to your church for its future.[3]

Now, let's be honest. Church volunteers are exhausted, too. You may not have as big a pool as you used to. It may be hard to staff current volunteer ministry positions, let alone develop new ones. Your church may have to make some choices about which ministries are viable now and which ones are not. You can initiate conversations about current capacity. Then notice how people respond—with curiosity, anger, or even relief.

The shift to a sustainable ministry pace for you and for others takes time. Some won't thank you, especially at first. It's a long-term project. You want to help people take responsibility for their church and its future.

When people are confident that practical matters are under control, they are more able to step up and embrace the bigger picture. Leadership and administration go hand in hand. When people know you are trustworthy in small matters, they will be more able to trust you in bigger ones. Show up when you say you will. Answer emails, texts, and voicemails within a reasonable time frame. (That doesn't necessarily mean *immediately*.)

Leadership and administration are related but not the same. Some people are geniuses at one but not the other. Even administratively gifted pastors can struggle to get things done now. Much has changed, staff members have turned over, and they themselves are worn out.

If you are not administratively gifted, you may need to find someone, paid or volunteer, to help you manage the details. Pastoral leaders often take too much responsibility for details. They may attend to all aspects of the worship service and the church office, even proofread the bulletin. In larger churches, they may have too many people reporting directly to them. They try to make sure all committees and teams are doing what they need to do. We'll talk more about how to manage the crush of practical demands in Chapter 7.

Third, your job *is* to recognize anxious behavior when you see it, in others, and in yourself. Anxiety goes with the territory of church leadership. Finding clarity about the forces at work in your church will help you navigate the anxiety in your church—and in you.

Whether you recognized it or not, you've seen anxiety in your congregation. Here are a few examples:

- Parking lot meetings (and, sometimes, private Zoom messages).

- Someone who sends a barrage of text messages at all hours.

- Someone who leaves the church without saying why then won't respond when you reach out.

- People who quit talking to each other because they disagree about (fill in the blank—COVID strategy, politics, the color of the new carpet).

And, believe it or not, someone who always says, "I'm with you, pastor, 100 percent!"

And you've experienced it yourself: You avoid your biggest critic. Your heart rate accelerates in a tough budget meeting. You don't reread an email blasting someone before sending it to them or to someone else.

When I talk about anxiety, I mean the ongoing chronic anxiety that is present in all living beings—and all systems made up of human beings. **Anxiety is part of life.** I think it's because we are mortal. We know our life is contingent. We won't live forever, and that kicks up anxiety. We all experienced real survival anxiety through the pandemic when lives really were in danger, but it's always there.

Murray Bowen defined *anxiety* as a response to a real or imagined threat. He also talked about what he called "chronic anxiety," that background anxiety that we all live with. We experience *acute anxiety* in the moment, perhaps when we have a close call on the freeway. The fight-or-flight response kicks in. Most of us, however, rarely face a real, physical threat—and yet we are anxious. We as individuals, as families, and as institutions have some level of background chronic anxiety. For Bowen, this was not a "syndrome" or diagnosis but something that all human beings experience. We acquire a certain amount of chronic anxiety growing up in our families of origin. For example, my own mother was the oldest child in a clergy family. My grandmother was anxious about how the family appeared to the church, and my mother felt pressure to be good and look good. While I didn't grow up in a clergy family, I also inherited some of that anxiety about being good and looking good.[4]

All churches are anxious systems. Put together in one place God, our certainties and uncertainties about matters of faith, numerous extended families, and money. The result is a pool of anxiety. Again, this is simply a fact, not a bad thing. It's a *good* thing that people gather in community to struggle with matters of faith and how to be together in a way that works. But it's not easy, and it's harder than it used to be. Add in institutional decline, a global pandemic, and ongoing political polarization. Anxiety inevitably has shot up.

Anxious behavior can show up in any number of ways. Sometimes you can observe people acting overtly anxious: sweating, breathing quickly, raising their voice. However, anxiety can also show up as a hyper-rational argument without any apparent emotion. Or in people who always agree with you, no matter what you say. Some of these behaviors are more difficult to deal with than others. Most pastors love having people agree with them. I know I did. However, knee-jerk compliance can be as anxiety-driven as knee-jerk disagreement. I've sat through congregational business meetings where everyone voted to pass a big budget deficit without a single question.

Anxiety Gets Focused on Particular Issues

Certain issues in congregational life are natural focuses for anxiety. People often get upset about them. Both music and ministry with children/youth are typical anxiety magnets. Rabbi Edwin Friedman used to say, "Lucifer jumped out of heaven and into the church choir." If you don't have a choir, it may be your worship team. Of course, sexuality and money are also easy focuses for anxiety. Sometimes they get combined: a fight about the youth ministry budget or an affair between the music director and a choir member.

When you can recognize these forces, the inevitable conflict will surprise you less. Most of us begin as idealistic new pastors who think that leading the church is going to be wonderful. Then the first fight happens, and we don't know what hit us. The last years have awakened many clergy to how people behave when they are anxious. In one case, a pastor experienced relentless criticism from her small church. She heard from a colleague who had received flowers from her grateful congregation. This pastor sent *herself* flowers to keep herself going, knowing her church would never express their appreciation. Their default anxious response was to criticize her. She was able to recognize this and find ways to take care of herself through some tough months.

Even when you see over-the-top nasty behavior, step back and ask yourself if it is possible that anxiety is at work. That alone may help lower *your* anxiety and think through how to address it.

Fourth, your work is also to find some space and time to think and rest. You can't provide the bigger picture or handle the administrative crush if you are exhausted. Kirk Byron Jones says, "The scripture does not say, be busy and know that I am God, but the scripture says, be still." Jones suggests a practice he calls morning B.R.E.W.: Be still. Receive God's Love. Embrace personhood. Welcome the day.[5] Whatever your preferred spiritual and Sabbath practices are, they are part of your work. As a pastor, I felt guilty at first about taking time for prayer at the office. Then I realized, this *is* my work, and I can't do the rest of the work without it.

What Your Work Is NOT

Your work is not to:

1. **Manage people's anxiety for them.** In fact, your job may be to treat them like grownups (even the ones who don't act like it) and push the penny of responsibility back across the table to them. For example, you can say, "I'm not sure how we can encourage families with children to come back. A lot of churches are struggling with this. What do you think?"

2. **Manage their relationships for them.** People are responsible for their own relationships.

3. **Keep them happy in general, and happy with you, in particular.** Leadership means you may have to make decisions that upset some people. Their upset *may* be a sign you are on the right track. In times like these it's impossible to keep everyone happy. You probably already know that. Part of your own work may be to increase your tolerance for people being upset with you.

4. **Guarantee their future.** You don't have that much power. You have a role to play and work to do, but their future is up to them and to God.

Lead from Yourself

One final word about what your work IS: Your work is to lead from your truest self. Your work requires your own emotional and spiritual growth. Always remember, **you are your biggest gift to your congregation.** The more you lead out of your deepest self, the better leader you will be. This doesn't mean saying, "That's just how I am," or, "That's just what I want." It doesn't mean you ignore feedback. But it also doesn't mean you constantly adapt yourself to your congregation and what it wants. Trying to keep them happy is not in their best interests or yours. Your own work at being principled but not rigid, and open but not a pushover will, over time, offer potential for productive ministry together.

What your people need (whether they know it or not) is a leader who is clear, self-defined, and able to manage him or herself in relationships. When you find a way to connect who you are with who they are, you have the most long-term potential for productive ministry. We'll talk as we go about how to put your wants, desires, and vision out to the congregation and what to do when individuals or groups react, as they inevitably will.

This approach to leadership involves what Murray Bowen described as differentiation of self, a foundational concept of Bowen theory. Bowen saw the variation in how people function in life and used this concept to describe what he observed. People at higher levels of differentiation have a wider repertoire than those who are less mature. They are more able to handle life challenges. They are more able to be clear about their own beliefs, without attacking those of others. Those at lower levels are more vulnerable to stress and less resilient physically and emotionally in the face of challenge. They are more reactive to others and to views that differ from their own. Every church contains people at a range of levels.[6] You can confirm this by observing any church discussion. Notice who is able to say consistently, "Here's what I think," and who says, "You should [fill in the blank.]." When people are more able to take responsibility for themselves and less likely to blame others, it indicates a higher level of differentiation.

Bowen suggested that the process of differentiation of self is ongoing (not a goal that is reached). It includes a person's work to become "sure of self on all life principles that involve himself [*sic*] and his family, to have the courage to take action on his convictions, and to devote primary attention to becoming the most responsible possible person."[7]

For pastoral leaders, that means you (1) work to be clear about your own principles about yourself and your ministry; (2) take action on those principles, even when you know others will disagree; and (3) are clear your job is first of all to be responsible in your role and your relationships with your people. That's a full-time job in and of itself, quite apart from the sermons, pastoral calls, and meetings.

In the next chapter, we'll look at how you can get connected with others and navigate the complex relationships in your ministry setting. We'll go deeper on what is and isn't your job in relation to the people you minister to and with.

Questions for Reflection

What do you love to do most in ministry? Are you doing any of that now (even a little)? Could you do more (even a little)?

What are your two or three most important ministry principles?

What are the (1) leadership and (2) administrative responsibilities of your role?

What are the favorite focuses for anxiety in your setting? (Music? Children? Declining participation?)

What are your ongoing and immediate strategies for managing your own anxiety?

What can you do to leave the outcome to God? Spiritually? Emotionally? Practically?

3

Get Connected

Who Do You Need to Relate To?

Therefore encourage one another and build up each other, as indeed you are doing.

—I THESS. 5:11 (NRSV)

My father came to faith in his thirties and was active in church for most of the rest of his life. He was a leader for a number of those years. Late in his life, he had some dementia. He could never remember what I did. He would say, "What is it you do?" And I would say, "I help pastors handle their biggest ministry challenges." He would ask, "What *is* the biggest challenge pastors have now?" Then before I could answer, he would say, "People, right?" And I would say, "Right, Dad."

People can be the biggest challenge *and* the biggest blessing in ministry. Whatever the mix in your ministry setting, getting connected and staying connected is a big part of the job. Relationships are essential to ministry: no relationships = no ministry.

In this chapter, we'll look at four important aspects of relationships. First, strategically building relationships to support your leadership. Second, navigating the reciprocal balance of responsibility in relationships. Third, how emotional triangles work and how you can manage yourself in them. And last but not least, how to respond when people criticize you.

Strategically Build Relationships to Support Your Leadership

Relationships are critical for moving the ministry forward. If you aren't connected enough to the people you are leading, you won't accomplish much. It's not just about your big ideas for the congregation, no matter how brilliant they are. You can't even develop the right ideas if you don't know your people.

- If you are new to a congregation, *connect.*

- If you want to get something going, *connect.*

- If the heat is on, *connect.*

- If you're about to go on sabbatical, or have just returned, *connect.*

How? Use a variety of ways to develop relationships, digital or the old-fashioned way, virtual or in-person. The most time-consuming—and the most valuable—are in-person conversations. Writing actual cards and notes also has a big impact since they are rare now. However, electronic options can also have a significant impact. One Baptist pastor who was about to go on sabbatical started texting members for their birthdays. He kept it up until sabbatical and started up again as soon as he got back. He heard over and over again how much people appreciated it.

If there is a hot issue in the congregation, you don't necessarily have to talk about it. You can simply make a pastoral connection with someone, or talk about a neutral topic. When I was a pastor in Massachusetts, talking about Red Sox baseball was a great way to cultivate relationships with the men in my church.

Edwin Friedman suggested clergy reach out to board members at least once in between meetings. This keeps the relationship going beyond church business. I found it useful to have a mental checklist of leaders. For example, I would ask myself, "Have I talked with the moderator this month? The chair of the executive board? How many deacons?" At coffee hour, you can scan the room to see who's there that you can touch base with quickly.

Pastoral care contacts enhance your position as a leader. Pastoral care is valuable for its own sake. You don't want to view people as simply instrumental to your plans. You don't respond to a pastoral need just because you need someone's support for an initiative. Yet the relationships you develop through pastoral care can make a difference to how people respond to your leadership.

You can't spend extended time with everyone in your congregation, unless you serve a very small congregation. You have to make choices. It's easy to spend hours with the neediest members of your church. They have frequent crises. They show up at church without an appointment and expect your attention. They don't have a good sense of time and may talk to you as long as you'll talk to them. Instead, I recommend you spend more time with the most mature in your congregation.

Ministry does mean being open to all kinds of people. It means being present with people in crisis. Sometimes you can't watch the clock; you simply have to be with folks. At the same time, I think of Edwin Friedman's frequent question, "Why are the least mature calling the shots?" He meant in church life and decision-making. However, it also applies to how you use your time and whom you spend it with.

Maturity doesn't mean those who are the oldest. I'm talking about those who:

- Learn from their experience

- Can tolerate differences

- Say, "I disagree," rather than "How can you say that!"

- Have a sense of humor

- Can see the bigger picture

A 25-year-old may have these characteristics and an 85-year-old may not. These characteristics express personal maturity. When you see them, take note.

Why should you spend more time with these people than with others who seem truly needy? After all, they are self-sufficient. They don't ask for a lot of your time. If they take a role, they fulfill it without a lot of fuss.

It's an investment in the future. People who are more mature have potential. The fact that they can learn from their experiences means they will benefit the most from time spent with you. In addition, they will have the most to teach you out of the many lessons they have learned in the past, no matter their age. They are future leaders. If they have held leadership positions in the past, they will be more inclined to do it again if they have a solid relationship with you. If they haven't, you can cultivate them for future positions. You know you need a pool of talent, and time spent this way helps deepen it.

Second, it helps keep *you* going. It's much more enjoyable to spend time with the mature than the immature. A lunch with a leader like this can get you through a tough week. Ministry is hard, and you need support from people within your congregation as well as outside.

Don't complain to these people about other more difficult people. That's not a productive use of their wisdom. Instead, you can simply enjoy time with them. You can ask their opinion about something. You can tell them what you are thinking about an area of ministry and get their feedback.

One key member in a church I served was a neighbor of ours. Ethel was committed and thoughtful. She could hear me—and I could hear her. Occasionally she'd call me to go out for coffee, always at McDonald's. She gave me helpful but not overly critical feedback. Ethel was my mother's age, which probably helped me hear her. Her presence was a blessing.

Caveats:

Stay connected with key players even if they aren't all that mature. If your church has leaders, formal and informal, who don't function so well, stay in touch with them. Don't avoid them even if you want to.

Cover the pastoral care bases. Care for people in the congregation is an important part of ministry. Don't ignore people just because they are difficult. However, you don't have to do everything they want or spend as much time with them as they want.

Some churches don't have many people who are mature. In some congregations, there's not a critical mass of mature folks. You may want to think about how long you want to stay. In the meantime, look for the *most* mature, those who are at least somewhat more able to take responsibility for themselves.

You may say, I'm already overburdened. How can I make *more* time? You might experiment with something for a week or a month, like a text a day or a phone call a week. More importantly, you may be taking too much responsibility in other areas. Letting go of something may help you spend more time building relationships.

Who's Responsible?

A second key element in ministry relationships is the balance between overfunctioning and underfunctioning. Those of us who are highly responsible in ministry and in life can easily become resentful of those who aren't stepping up. We think, if they only would do their part, I wouldn't be so overburdened.

Bowen family systems theory includes the idea of overfunctioning and underfunctioning. The basic idea is this: There's a balance between those who take too much responsibility and those who don't take enough. It's not simply that those who don't do anything are "irresponsible." Instead, there's a reciprocal relationship between the two parties. When you get resentful, you do nothing to shift this balance. In fact, your resentment can solidify it further. Whether you seethe in silence or nag others to do their part, you perpetuate the pattern. For example, a long-time church administrator never quite gets the hang of the new church software system. Every month, she asks the pastor for help in running the monthly reports. The pastor internally seethes that she can't remember. But he goes ahead and helps her without saying anything. Underfunctioning administrator and overfunctioning pastor—it's reciprocal. It takes two to keep it going.

Most of us learn this overfunctioning-underfunctioning pattern in our families of origin. If you tend to overfunction, you might have had younger siblings to take care of. Or perhaps one of your parents wasn't quite up to the job and needed you to help carry the load. You might still have a family member who regularly calls on you for advice or financial help. The family may look to you to be the family chaplain and perform family weddings and funerals. You may be the functional social worker in finding resources for family members who need them.

Even chronically overfunctioning clergy can underfunction in some areas of family and church life. I was embarrassed when my car stalled and I didn't even know how to open the hood. Even though I tend to overfunction in my marriage, I had always let Karl take care of the cars. The reciprocity worked differently in that arena. I did step up a little after that incident and started taking my own car in for service.

Clergy can underfunction in some ways in church life, for example in relation to church finance and stewardship. They may intensely overfunction in every other area, but they avoid money conversations. Correspondingly, their finance leaders are happy to overfunction and have the minister stay out of "their business." (See Chapter 5 for more on money.)

Early in the pandemic clergy, staff, and a few leaders *had* to take on extra responsibility to adapt to the new reality. In a crisis, this wasn't overfunctioning, but necessary functioning. As time went on, in the adjustment to the hybrid environment, leaders put in a lot of ongoing effort.

In today's environment, there may be fewer people on hand to do what needs to be done. It's easy for clergy and staff to keep doing what they've been doing, even when they are in an overfunctioning relationship with the congregation.

You can't keep this going forever. What to do instead of continuing to overfunction:

1. Be clear about what you will and won't do.

2. Let go of resentment and focus on your clarity about what you will and won't do.

3. Decide whether to communicate what you will and won't do. Sometimes if you've been picking up the slack, you can simply stop doing so without a word. Other times it's important to make a statement. Be clear about what you want to say and choose a time in advance when you can be clear and calm.

4. Let go of the outcome, to the degree that you can. Be prepared for a lag time. Others won't step up until you step down, but there's usually a gap, and sometimes people never step up. Don't take it personally or be surprised by it.

You Can't Get Out of Triangles

Ministry relationships make more sense when you understand emotional triangles. Every ministry leader lives in triangles all the time. They are everywhere in church life.

What is a triangle? It's a three-person relationship system. Bowen called it "the smallest stable relationship system."[1] When anxiety increases between two people, one pulls in someone else to help handle the anxiety. For example, the custodian complains to the church administrator every Monday about the mess left by the A/V team on Sunday. The administrator doesn't oversee that team, but she feels anxious and as if she should do something about the problem. The custodian feels calmer because he has unloaded some of his anxiety. When the pastor comes in, the admin may tell her about what the custodian said, thus creating a triangle. The admin feels better, the pastor worse. The pastor wonders if *she* should do something about the problem.

There are some triangles that go with the job. You inherit these triangles when you say yes to the position. Examples of these are the triangle between you, the congregation, and your predecessor. Or you, the board, and the congregation. As long as you are in that church, you are part of those triangles. When you leave, you'll be in a triangle with your successor and the congregation.

It's important to remember that triangles aren't bad. They are part of human experience. If you reread the beginning of Genesis, you'll see the story where Adam says to God, "The woman tempted me." He blamed Eve for the sin God was calling him on. Triangle: Adam, Eve, God. Triangles go way back.

The approach to take is not to say, "I shouldn't be in triangles," or "I have to get out of this triangle." Rather, the question is, "How do I manage myself in the triangles I am part of?"

In ministry, people frequently pull you into triangles when they get anxious. Someone thinks the children need to be better behaved during worship. She says to you, "Pastor, don't you think the children are disruptive in worship? I think Patricia [children's ministry director] should do more to keep them quiet." Instead of involving Patricia, you might say, "I'm just happy the children are back! I don't care how much noise they make."

Or a member shares with you her concerns regarding her husband and his chronic underemployment. She is anxious about her financial security and looking for you to do something to help. She may even ask you to have a conversation with him, hoping that will get him into shape.

The work is to be in these triangles without being caught, without feeling it's up to you to fix things. Taking responsibility for other people's relationships is a form of overfunctioning. If you step in, you are taking on what does not belong to you. You bear the stress for a relationship you aren't even part of, whether it's a staff relationship or a marriage.

When you try to fix someone else's relationship, it doesn't work. In fact, the relationship can even get worse. No matter how well-intentioned our efforts, they can backfire. I see this when I'm coaching pastors who are dealing with feuding staff members. The more the pastor tries to mediate, the worse the relationship becomes.

If you are in these triangles all the time, what can you do? You can work on the relationships you are directly involved in. If the parishioner who complains about the children in worship is the board chair, you might connect with her more frequently on other matters. You don't have to give too much attention to her complaints about the children. You may find they subside. You might give some thought to your own principles about children in worship. You might coach the children's ministry director on how she can relate to that parishioner in a way that is less emotionally reactive to the complaints.

With staff members who are not getting along, you can clearly communicate what you will and won't tolerate. You can refuse to listen to one complain about the other. You can talk with each one instead about their own goals for their functioning and their leadership.

In pastoral care, you can work on your relationship with the parishioner who is talking to you. You may not have a relationship with her husband at all, or you may, if he is also in the congregation. Your task is to stay relatively neutral and not take her side. Remember, it always takes two to make a marriage or a marital problem.

There are even times when you can productively *create* triangles. For example, when you are being harassed by a church member, it's time to strategically triangle in other leaders. That's a positive use of triangles. "I just wanted you to know that Bob is calling me every evening to shout at me. I've told him I'm not going to answer my phone when he calls anymore." You can insist that others share the responsibility for handling the most challenging members. It's not all up to you.

The wonderful thing about congregational ministry is you get daily opportunities to practice. Triangles show up everywhere, with staff, members, and in your family.

Relating to Critics

Finally, important relationships in ministry are not solely with people who agree with you. Every pastoral leader gets criticism. Believe it or not, your critics are doing you a favor—even if you hate criticism.

First, your critics *may* give you a sign you are on the right track with your leadership. While most of us want everyone to stand up and cheer when we are proposing something new, that's not realistic. In fact, if everyone cheers, you probably haven't gone far enough. The "new" direction will keep the status quo, and that keeps everyone content.

Critics are a sign you really have upset the balance with what you are doing or are simply proposing. That upset is essential for progress. If everyone is happy, chances are the church is not moving forward.

Just because someone doesn't like it doesn't mean you are doing the wrong thing. Just the opposite may be true. You can even celebrate that you are experiencing criticism, even if emotionally you hate it. It's the price of progress. One pastor began to address issues of racial reconciliation from the pulpit for the first time. He got criticism from two sides. Some were outraged he brought it up at all. Others thought he didn't go far enough. He took that as an indication he'd come down in about the right place, for himself, and for that congregation.

Second, your critics can teach you about yourself. Become a student of your own reaction to your critics. Do you:

- Cringe?

- Want to run away?

- Want to defend yourself?

- Want to argue or fight?

- Want to change it back so they are happy?

- Go silent?

Think about your family and how criticism was or wasn't used. In my family, we didn't talk about difficult subjects openly. I have one colleague whose parents criticize the sermon over lunch when they visit. By contrast, the very last time my father heard me preach, he said, "I'm so proud of you." Is one way better than another? I don't know, but they are different. Because my mother rarely made critical comments, I still remember a few she did make, and how much they stung. When I got into ministry, I had to become less sensitive, and it wasn't easy.

Third, your critics can help you toughen up. Thick skin is a requirement for leadership. Many pastors don't have it. They go into ministry because they love and they want to be loved. They're used to attention from their parents. They may have been the special child in one way or another: oldest child, only boy/girl, most religious, best-behaved. In their heart of hearts, they still want attention. Then they are shocked by the realities of church leadership.

I met a pastor with a background in law enforcement who went into a tough congregation. The choir turned their backs on him once in the worship service. However, he survived and went on to have a productive and thriving ministry there. I asked him if his secular work experience helped him in his ministry. He said, "Every day." I wish I'd asked him about his family background.

Before COVID, many clergy didn't have the experience of working in a truly tough environment. The pandemic opened many pastors' eyes to what church people can get up to. The current environment means that behavior that used to be unacceptable at church has now become acceptable in some churches. I know of one pastor who received a critical letter made up of cut-out, pasted-down letters.

Another pastor received call after call from members shouting at him about the COVID restrictions. You may be worn down by what's come your way over the last few years. You may be saying, "Enough already!"

Sometimes you have to take a clear stand with individuals who are behaving badly. You can simply say early on, as Israel Galindo recommends, "I know what you are doing, and it needs to stop." If the situation is escalating, you can't do it alone. You must have allies among the lay leadership. Another Friedman line is: "I can leave, but you are still going to have to deal with these people." I like this response because it helps get you on the other side of fear for your job. It also pushes the responsibility for the congregation back where it belongs, on congregational leadership.

You can't control the ultimate outcome. For us pastors, it's terribly hard to let go of our Messiah complex. We really do want to save the world, including our possibly not-too-functional congregation. Some churches will always let the saboteurs win. If you are the fifth pastor to face down the same crowd, it's not about you. Other churches have enough substance and health to make it through a crisis and move to a higher level of functioning. Ministry always involves assessing potential in individuals and in congregations. Paradoxically, the freer you are about whether or not your efforts at differentiated leadership "work," the more potential there may be.

Pray, do your best and leave the rest to God. And it's always worth it if you learn something.

Finally, it's easy to focus on the problems. It's worth regularly taking the time to notice what's going right.

Questions for Reflection

Where might you be taking responsibility for other people's relationships? How can you step back?

What is your purpose for developing relationships in the congregation?

Whom do you want to spend more time with? Less time?

What are ways you respond when people criticize you? What other options do you see?

What do you appreciate about the people in your congregation?

4

Get Reflective
Who Are You?

Or how can you say to your neighbor, "Let me take the speck out of your eye," while the log is in your own eye?

—MATT. 7:4 (NRSV)

My friend Rev. Kent Harrop, an American Baptist pastor near Boston, called his Aunt Evelyn early in the COVID shutdown to check in. She said she was doing fine, then added, "It's not my first worldwide pandemic!" He thought she was a little confused, and then he realized she meant the early twentieth-century flu pandemic the year she was born. She said, "If the first one didn't get me, this one's not going to get me. I have a great-grandson I want to get to know." He reflected at the time, "That helps me when I get whiny." Aunt Evelyn lived next door to him when he was growing up. She was a refuge from a difficult home life and has been an ongoing resource for him throughout his life. The last time I asked him, "How's Aunt Evelyn?" he answered, "She just turned 107!"[1]

Most pastors don't realize exploring their family story and learning more about what makes them tick can be as beneficial as a host of ministry workshops. When you know yourself in this deep way, both your strengths and your trigger points, you will be a better leader. You'll find your own direction for ministry more easily. You'll be clearer about where you end and other people begin. You'll have more compassion for others, who also have complex stories. And you'll be able to connect more thoughtfully with those who think and behave differently than you. You may even find wisdom to get you through the next global crisis.

Why Family?

Why is it worth the time and energy to explore your family of origin? We all learn to relate to others in the family we grow up in. We learn our initial lessons on the meaning of life, work, money, and faith from the people who raise us.

If you can bring a thoughtful presence to an intense situation, you probably learned something about it in your family. If you have good business sense, you may have absorbed important facts from a parent in business. If you know how to include others who are left out, you probably learned that at home, too.

On the other hand, if you find conflict difficult, you likely learned that in your family. People may have experienced a lot of destructive conflict—or avoided conflict at all costs. If you hate talking openly about money, you learned that lesson from your family, one way or another. If you hate being left out, you may have learned that in your family, by being someone's confidante and learning to like that. Or maybe you were always left out and longed to be inside.

Your greatest strengths and challenges come from the family you grew up in. Learning to be more reflective and more neutral about your family, its history, and its members can help you access the strengths of your family. You can also gain perspective on some of the challenges you inherited.

How does that help you in your ministry? For one thing, you may find a clone of the family member you are most reactive to in every church you serve. If you move to another ministry, you'll find another one. (And if that person leaves the church you are in now, someone else will join the church to take their place.) If you can tone down your allergy to whatever in these people sets you off, you'll be more effective and less stressed in your ministry. When you can reconnect with your family and learn to be less reactive there, you will become less reactive at church. You may think *I could never do that*. However, even a little more neutrality and calm go a long way, both in the family and in ministry.

One pastor served several churches where a key male leader was always problematic for her. Sometimes it was the president of the congregation, sometimes the treasurer. But there was always someone. When she reflected on her family, she realized that her reactivity to these men was related to her relationship with her father. He was extremely directive and not happy that she had gone into ministry. Not only that, but her mother also had a conflicted relationship with her own father. This awareness alone helped her be calmer in the relationship with "the one" in her current congregation. In addition, she started connecting with her father, separate from conversations with her mother. Her grandfather had died, but she started asking her mother more questions about him and how her mother related to him.

You may find clones of different family members in different congregations. For example, Rev. Katie Long says, "In my first church, I dealt with someone who was childish in ways my grandmother, who came at the end of a large family and lived with us, was." Long adds, "In a later congregation, I had a treasurer who was as set on being in control as my father was (after a childhood when he couldn't control much.) After much family work by then, I was able to broaden control of the finances without his losing face."[2]

What Is This Work?

Family process work is more complicated than anything I can summarize in one brief chapter. Essentially, it is taking a step back and looking at your family as a whole. This work is based on understanding that what happens between family members is more important than what happens in any one person. Family problems, including symptoms in any family member, arise out of the complex of relationships. Symptoms can take many forms: emotional, physical, social. They are not due to just one immediate family member, but to patterns in the extended family and over generations.[3] I frequently quote Edwin Friedman's line, "The problem with parents is they had parents."

The work itself is learning to be more of a "self" in the family you grew up in, to be clear about your own convictions, beliefs, and functioning. And to stay in touch with others in the family without trying to convince them of anything or change them.

Clergy often face two challenges:

1) They think they don't have anything "in common" with members of their family who don't have the same interests or values, so they avoid them. That tendency has intensified as polarization in America has increased.

2) When they do engage, they find it hard to do so without trying to help, change, or convince others of their point of view. They share their ideas for things family members should do "for their own good."

I have come to realize over the years that my automatic stance that I am right or that I know what's best for someone else doesn't actually help. It gets in the way of genuine, mature relationships. Whether in my family or at church, when I can simply take a stand for myself and give others room to be themselves, everything goes better. And I'm less stressed and happier.

In addition, looking at the multigenerational patterns in your family can give you a clearer perspective on why they are the way they are. You can see that it's not just your brother John who struggles to stand on his own feet financially, but also Uncle Charlie and Great-Uncle Fred, and even Great-Great-Uncle Sam. Then you may be less judgmental and more compassionate about John (and maybe Uncle Charlie, too).

You may come to see your parents as two human beings who did the best they could under circumstances that may have been difficult indeed. To the degree you can, you will be more able to show compassion and be less reactive to those in your congregation who seem the most troublesome. This doesn't mean that you simply give in to troublesome family members or church members. You still may have to take a stand, but you can do it with a different energy.

What You Can Learn from Your Multigenerational Family

Your multigenerational family is a great learning resource. This is not a "once and done" project. Rather, it's a learning process you can explore for the rest of your life. You can learn infinite lessons from your family. Here are a few to reflect on:

1. You can learn how to be resilient. If you are alive, you and your family are survivors. Your ancestors did not succumb to disease, hunger, or violence. If you had a challenging childhood, you have already learned to be a survivor. Without negating any of the pain you may have experienced, I want to lift up the reality that you got something out of it. You learned to be cagey or silent or bold or "good" or "bad." You figured out how to survive.

On my mother's side, my great-grandparents moved from Nebraska to California with eight children from toddlers to teenagers in the early twentieth century. Why did they leave? Why California? I don't know, but I am in awe.

What do you know about your grandparents or great-grandparents? What obstacles did they face and how did they survive them? In some families this information is hard to get; in others the stories are told all the time (and some of them are true . . .).

2. **You can learn how to connect with people across difference.** Every family has to deal with difference. Even families with a lot of similarity who stay in the same place have members who are more or less successful, more or less religious, or more or less compliant.

Where are the differences in your family and how have people dealt with them? Openly? By cutting off? By pretending they don't exist? As you learn about the branches of the family that are most different from your own and connect with the living members of those branches, you have an unparalleled opportunity for growth.

Some years ago, I visited a cousin on my dad's side, an elk hunter. I had just come from a retreat at a Trappist monastery. We both agreed that it was more likely that I would go elk hunting than that he would go on a retreat in a monastery. Edwin Friedman had once asked me, "Who's going to teach you how to be mean?" I didn't think it was possible. Well, this cousin is a retired state police officer, and he is one tough guy. Many people experience him as mean. I have a built-in teacher in my own family.

Which of the "different" people in your family, for example, the outsiders, can teach you something you need to know about life?

3. **You can learn to be curious rather than judgmental.** This relates to #2. You may come from a judgmental family, of course. If you step back and look at the multigenerational patterns in your family, your curiosity can be piqued. See if there's someone else in the family who is a little bit outside the swirling currents but not cut off from them. Seek them out, and over time pick their brain a bit. What do they notice about the family patterns? One pastor interviewed all his cousins and learned new perspectives on his parents and the entire family.

You don't have to do formal "interviews." If you are new at this, it's better to keep it casual. Simply show up at family milestones: weddings, funerals, reunions. Try not to be the officiant if you can help it. Step back and see what you notice about how people relate to each other. Watch your own negative thoughts. For example, you may have an automatic thought like, "Uncle Fred is impossible!" Those thoughts may actually not be your own. They may be inherited observations internalized from your parents over a lifetime.

Can you see challenging family members as part of a larger system? Each generation may have an Uncle Fred. There's often a spot open for someone "impossible" for some reason. See if you can figure out what "impossible" means. Angry? Determined? Less social than everyone else—or more?

In your curious exploration, avoid asking "why." Become an observer and see if you can figure out "who," "what," "when," and "where." People's behavior and relationship patterns always have multiple causes. The origin of the pattern may be lost in the mists of time. In your exploring, you may find some big events, great celebrations, or great traumas that contributed to the patterns. However, even these feed into a larger complex of factors. Some families recover quickly from trauma, others don't. It's not just the event itself.

Cultivating curiosity and moving away from judgment will help you considerably at church. It's easy to have a whole stream of judgmental thoughts about difficult individuals and to label and blame others. Instead, step back, observe, and learn.

I've found that this work, as challenging as it can be, is well worth it. It's helped me have greater freedom in all my relationships, both inside and outside the family. I've been at it for over three decades, so it's not a quick fix. But the "fix" has substance and staying power.

How Do You Do It?

This is simply an introductory summary. I strongly recommend you find a family-systems-trained coach. You can also join one of the clergy leadership training programs I recommend in the Resources section at the end of this book. I'll recommend some books as well. It's hard to do this work from a book, let alone a few brief words like these. However, reading books can help you get started. That's how I did it, using Harriet Lerner's *The Dance of Anger* and *The Dance of Intimacy*.[4] (The Resources list has suggested books.) Later I did more work with a coaching group in Friedman's training program for clergy, and then with an individual therapist/coach.

I recommend starting with a family diagram covering at least three generations. You can use software or do it by hand.[5] *A Family Genogram Workbook*[6] offers information about creating a family diagram. It includes great questions to ask about your family.

Murray Bowen suggested three specific elements of this work, what he called "principles and techniques." These are far more than "how to"; they offer a way to approach relationships over a lifetime.

1. **Develop person-to-person relationships.** As I said above, this means one-to-one. It can be hard to pry "Mom-and-Dad" out into separate relationships. You might try calling them at work or at a time when the other is out or away. If they each have their own cell phone, it helps (but not if they are never apart or always put it on speaker so the

other one can hear). "If you can get a person-to-person relationship with each living person in your extended family, it will help you 'grow up' more than anything else you could ever do in life."[7]

2. **Become a better observer and control your own emotional reactiveness.** We learned those automatic reactions before we could even remember, so this isn't easy. It involves taking one or two steps back to observe the patterns in your family. You may have to work hard to stay off the usual script everyone in the family already knows. ". . . [getting] 'beyond blaming' and 'beyond anger' to a level of objectivity that is far more than an intellectual exercise."[8]

3. **Detriangle yourself from emotional situations.** This means avoiding being on someone's side, being more neutral in the family triangles. You can't get out of those triangles, but you can live in them differently. We so automatically take someone's side that we don't even know we're doing it. Isn't it obvious Mom is the heroine and Dad is the villain? The full story is always more complicated. The multigenerational view can help us see this. Where are the "heroines" and "villains" in earlier generations?

"The overall goal is to be constantly in contact with an emotional issue involving two other people and self, without taking sides, without counterattacking or defending self, and to always have a neutral response."[9]

This is an ongoing process of observation and connection over time. I find these three principles continually useful. They help me relate more responsibly to my husband, my brother, my extended family, and my adult children. My job is not to explain or defend anyone to anyone else.

Of course, you can engage in these practices at church, too. You will find plenty of opportunities to work on person-to-person relationships, become a better observer, and avoid taking sides in the inevitable triangles.

How Long Does It Take?

Most people can find some immediate benefit from taking a more neutral look at their family. I've coached many people on this process, and I can see that they can find some short-term gains early on. For example, people commonly quickly see their compulsive overfunctioning. They realize that taking responsibility for others has a price for them and for the others.

However, I think this is a lifetime's work. That's good news and bad news. The bad news is that it's a big challenge to lean into your family story. You are never done with this work. The good news is you don't have to get it right all at once. There's always more to work with. Your family is always there. If everyone is dead, you can find out more information about them. You can visit graves or connect with more distant relatives or meet people who are or were important to the family.

I've been exploring my family, its strengths and challenges, for 35 years. I have continued to learn new things about the family and people in it, even those closest to me. A few years before my father died in 2020, we had a conversation about his sales career. We were going to the doctor and arrived early. He said, "You don't want to hurry." He then said about sales calls, "It's okay if you wait for them, but you don't want them to wait for you." He paused and added, "It's a disciplined life." He was in his nineties, and I had never heard him talk about that aspect of his work before. It was a gift.

As I thought about it, I realized ministry is also a disciplined life on many levels. We make and keep appointments, complete worship preparation and sermons, keep track of administrative details. I always thought my mother was the one who gave me those gifts (and she was good at it). I always had the perspective my dad wasn't good at keeping track of details because she did it so well. I see now that he had more organizational strengths than I thought. He played his part in the gifts of discipline I bring to my ministry. I'm grateful for that conversation. We had it more than 20 years after I began to engage with him in a different way, working to be more curious and less judgmental.

Why Bother?

What are the long-term benefits? It seems like a lot of work, and it is. It can be painful and difficult. I strongly recommend, again, that you find someone to work with who can help you. We are all too close to our families to get perspective. If you take this on, every chapter in this book will have more value for you. Learning to manage yourself better and be less reactive in your family relationships can have immediate benefits at church. You'll have more choices, be calmer, clearer, and overall a better leader. It's not a magic bullet, and it's not easy work. But it's important work.

I have coached a number of pastors over many years, not only on ministry matters but also to help them reflect on their family of origin. What I observe in them is greater calm and clarity, less reactivity and anxiety. They experience more enjoyment both of their families and their life in ministry. There's no quick fix. Sometimes it may seem like a slog. The work is difficult for everyone. In addition, some families are extraordinarily anxious, complex, and challenging. However, the good news is this: There's always some more work to do, some new avenue to explore that can help you navigate relationships in every setting.

If you have children, the best thing you can do for them is work on yourself in the context of your family. This can keep you from getting overly focused on your kids in a way that doesn't benefit them. It can help you be part of passing along the strengths and short-circuiting at least some of the negativity that all families have. If you don't have children, the work is a contribution to the following generations in your wider family.

There are plenty of opportunities to get reflective every day in ministry. Can you become a student of yourself and your own reactions? When you can't see straight about something, chances are the trigger comes from something in your family of origin. The more you can focus on yourself and your own functioning and responses, rather than blaming others, the better off you are. Why? You can do something about your own response. And a systems approach means this: If you change yourself, something changes in the relationship. You may get a different response from others.

Tips for exploring your family story:

- Make short visits. It's hard to maintain your equilibrium for more than three days.

- Talk one-on-one when possible. You may know about Jewish philosopher Martin Buber's "I-Thou" relationship. Buber used this phrase to describe a mature, mutual relationship between individuals. It's a challenge to work on that in a big group.[10]

- Visit cemeteries. It's a way to connect with people who are no longer living.

- Collect data and watch for patterns. Think of this as a research project.

- Use church conferences or continuing education as an opportunity to connect with extended family nearby. It lowers the ante ("I'll be in the area."). You can get together for a meal instead of a long visit. Extra bonus: It's cheaper.

- Take the long view (forward and backward). Your family has been shaped over many generations. Both the strengths and challenges have deep roots. Your exploration of the story is a long-term effort.

- Get coaching or other support. Some systems workshops offer coaching as part of the program. (See Resources.)

Getting Support for Your Reflection on Yourself

Getting reflective about yourself in ministry is an ongoing practice. Professional help, paid or unpaid, is a critical form of ministry support. You have doubtless already faced challenges that seemed too much for you. When you feel out of your depth about something at church, if you can't sleep or can't think, it's time to reach out. Several different kinds of people can help you get perspective on your ministry and keep going.

There's no getting around the fact that ministry is lonely. On one level, you must become comfortable with that fact. However, that doesn't mean you have to go it completely alone when you face a big challenge or ongoing difficulties in your everyday work. Instead, find people outside the congregation who can help you step back, think through options, and develop maturity in ministry.

I've used a wide range of professionals at different times in my ministry. It's been worth every hour and every cent I've spent on the phone, face to face, and virtually. They have helped me walk through challenging times in my individual, family, and professional life. I'm not sure I'd still be in ministry of any kind without their support.

Colleagues. The right colleagues can be a great support for you. This won't cost you anything; however, you want to choose carefully.

My friend Cindy Maybeck and I attended Rabbi Friedman's clergy training program together 30 years ago. We ate up his ideas. Then we helped each other deepen our learning and put it into practice in our churches and our families. We have continued to talk and coach each other informally. We live on opposite sides of the country now, but I still call and say, "I could use some help thinking this through . . ." I called her last week with a family challenge. I was second-guessing myself. She said, "No, you're not overfunctioning. That's important for you to do." Because we share a framework and know each other's history, she can be consistently helpful. I hope I do the same for her.

You want to choose someone who is thoughtful, not overly reactive, and able to challenge you and not just commiserate. When I was tempted to step back into a crisis while on sabbatical, I called Cindy. She said, "If you go back, you will undo all the boundary work you did before you left." This was good advice. She helped me to stay on track with my plan.

Mentors. You may already have a relationship with a more experienced pastor. As with colleagues, choose someone who is mature, able to stay calm, and able to challenge you as well as provide support. Some people develop formal mentor-mentee relationships. As a younger pastor, I simply had a few older colleagues who could give me counsel when needed. I still have enormous respect for them, including those who are now gone. They remain alive in their influence on my life and ministry today.

Coaches. I define a *coach* as someone who can help you think through a situation, move toward your goals, and respond thoughtfully to ministry challenges. Some coaches are certified, but some of the best I know are not.

My coaches have served a couple of different roles. First, they have been accountability partners for areas of my life I'm working on personally and professionally. They have helped me keep on track with priorities. Second, some have helped talk me down when something happened where I was too close to see options. My coaches have asked questions and brought perspective. They have helped me see I had choices and that even the worst that could happen was something I could handle. They have offered space to take a breath, step down from the fight-or-flight response, and think rather than simply react.

Therapists. Fortunately, the stigma about seeing a therapist is not what it used to be. If you are doing sustained work on family of origin, having a guide will be a big help. The same is true if you are having a personal or marital crisis. If you have a child with problems of any kind, I recommend you go yourself before you take your child. Working on yourself is the best thing you can do for your child.

My bias is toward working with someone trained in Bowen family systems theory. My reason: This approach looks at the larger relationship system rather than trying to "fix" any one individual, including the client. I find it offers more potential for growth than other approaches because of this long-term, big-picture perspective. I continue to find it rich and compelling for me and for the pastors I work with.

Spiritual Directors. I'll talk about this resource in Chapter 8, "Get Prayerful."

Continuing Education. Much ministry continuing education is focused on such techniques for ministry as becoming a better preacher. That's important, of course. I'm talking about something else, though. Some clergy development programs focus on developing yourself, not simply your skills. See the Resources at the end of the book for programs that use Bowen theory to help you reflect professionally and personally.

A few don'ts:

1. **Don't go it alone.** It's not possible to sustain the stresses of ministry alone and maintain your well-being for a year, let alone for a career.

2. **Don't rely solely on your spouse if you are married.** His or her anxiety is bound to be up if yours is. The wife of one

pastor in crisis I was coaching knew from her husband that we were working together. She told me, "I'm so glad he has you. It was getting to be too much for me." Your spouse may get defensive for you, angry with you, or both. Spouses can't be consistently neutral.

3. **Don't rely solely on church staff or members.** You need an outside perspective.

4. **Don't rely on "clergy support groups" that are nothing but complaint sessions.** They won't help you grow.

If you don't have *any* support outside the congregation, pick at least one of the options above to help you get reflective. If you already have someone, you may need to add another type of resource person. If you don't know where to go, ask your friends. If you try someone and it doesn't work out, don't give up. Through all the ups and downs of ministry life, you **will** need some additional support. You are too close to your life and ministry to have enough perspective on it, especially when the heat is on.

Questions for Reflection

Where do you see strength and resourcefulness in your family of origin?

In what ways has your family shaped you to do the work you've chosen? What was the place of faith in the family over the generations?

Who are the different people in your family, the outsiders? Who is living that you could connect with? How might you do that?

What are you curious about in your family? Where might you explore that curiosity?

Think about a current troubling matter in your ministry setting. Are there clues from your family story as to what is a trigger point for you in this issue or these relationships?

Who are the support people in your life? Write them down. What additional support might you need?

5

Get to the Money
What Is Your Role?

And God is able to provide you with every blessing in abundance,
so that by always having enough of everything, you may share
abundantly in every good work.

— II COR. 9:8 (NRSV)

A *New Yorker* cartoon shows a tycoon standing at the gates of heaven. St. Peter says to him, "You had more money than God. That's a big no-no."[1] It makes me laugh every time. When I was a pastor, I had a file of cartoons about money that I liked to review before trustees' meetings. It helped me lighten up. I walked into the meetings feeling more relaxed and ready for the conversations.

If you find yourself anxious about money matters, take heart. You are not alone. Nowadays, even churches that never worried about money find their financial future uncertain. Many churches know their biggest givers won't be around in 10 years. Younger generations may never give at the same level. Some major givers didn't come back to church when services resumed. Some of them are still giving, but you're not sure it's good for the church to be supported by people who never participate in worship. Churches that were on the financial edge earlier are facing a crunch, if not a crisis.

Money can be a challenging topic for clergy for a variety of reasons:

- You feel inadequate because you weren't trained to deal with it.

- You feel defensive because people's giving pays your salary.

- Other people think they know more than you do (and sometimes they do).

- Giving patterns are changing, and you and your lay leaders are not sure what to do about it. What used to work isn't working anymore.

- You grew up in a family where money was never discussed openly.

- It seems a little "dirty," not spiritual.

However, like it or not, dealing with money is part of your job. Even if it's your least favorite part of ministry, keep reading! It took me years to get comfortable leading in this area.

Things That Matter

Five things matter in relation to money: money itself, anxiety, leadership, relationships, and history. Remembering each will help you lead in this important area of ministry.

Money Matters

It takes resources to do ministry. This is not a bad thing. It's just a fact. You can confidently take leadership in this area because it's essential to ministry (see next point). Paul says, "Each of you must give as you have made up your mind, not reluctantly or under compulsion, for God loves a cheerful giver" (2 Cor. 8:7, NRSV). He's talking about a collection for the poorer church in Jerusalem. However, he never hesitated to ask people to give to support ministry.

Money is not the most important thing, of course. Growing disciples is our most important task. These disciples can make a difference in the world through sharing the gospel in word and deed. Ministry has been done on a shoestring for centuries, but even Jesus had patrons, the wealthy women who supported his ministry.

Christian theology suggests that money itself is not dirty. Remember, it's not money that's the "root of all evil," but "the love of money" (I Tim 6:10). An incarnational theology suggests that the physical world is touched by the holy, not just the so-called "spiritual" world. Many Christians have had trouble with that over the centuries, in relation to sex, the arts, and money. Humanity and the church itself desperately need to see the holy at the heart of our bodily life, including our money. When money flows into the church and out for ministry, something holy is happening. Both the inflow and the outflow are important. We don't need to apologize for this to ourselves or to others.

Anxiety Matters

We talked about anxiety and leadership in Chapter 2. Money is a particularly high-anxiety topic. (Stop me if you are surprised . . .) We need money to survive. Biologically, we need money for food and shelter. When money is scarce, our survival instincts kick into overdrive. It's harder to think creatively, to imagine new ways of doing things. Many congregations are naturally conservative (whatever their theology). They can insist even more than usual, "We've never done it that way before."

If you underestimate the loaded nature of money in congregational and individual life, the way people react can shock you. When you offer a novel way to balance the budget, people act as if you are proposing to demolish the sanctuary. Or you suggest that perhaps the pastor should know who gives how much. Then someone suggests that perhaps they need a new pastor.

Anxiety can even cause us to stop the flow of money into and out of the church in various ways:

- Not asking people to give out of fear they will get upset.

- Accumulating more resources than we need. Endowments can be useful for funding ministry into the future. But when churches refuse to spend the "rainy day" fund when it's obviously "raining," leaders are making an anxious decision.

- Avoiding hard decisions or making them too quickly (refusing to make necessary budget cuts or taking a slash-and-burn approach at the first sign of a shortfall).

- Cutting mission/outreach giving as a first resort.

Now, anxiety isn't all bad. Peter Steinke said in an interview I did with him some years ago:

> [Anxiety] can be a motivator. It can help us see that what we are doing and where we are going may not be where we should be. And, therefore, anxiety can help us make some changes. The problem with anxiety is when it becomes intense and protracted. Then, rather than promoting some change, it paralyzes us.[2]

These four tips can help you deal with financial anxiety in the congregation and yourself:

1. **Recognize it in others.** You don't necessarily have to tell people, "It's just anxiety at work." Still, knowing something may be going on with others can help you stay calm when people say things or make decisions that don't seem rational. About relating to others who are anxious about money (or anything else), Steinke said, "I have to focus on my functioning. I cannot focus on their functioning, so I cannot take it as my task to make them less anxious. There is very little I am going to do about it anyway, especially with the chronically anxious who get anxious about anything and everything. But do I allow their anxiety to stir up mine, or can I stay outside of the circumference of their anxiety?"

2. **Recognize it in yourself.** Being aware of your own anxiety will help you have more choices. You know how your body and mind react—sweaty palms, beating heart, the desire to cut and run or fight it out. Use your own anxiety as a signal to stop and pay attention rather than simply react.

3. **Breathe.** The best way to calm yourself down in the moment is to take deep breaths. Try this: Before a budget meeting, take a

deep breath and hold it for five seconds, then let it out. Then repeat. Neuropsychologist Angelo Bolea said this helps prepare your brain to receive new information.[3] So you may notice something new in the meeting or have a new idea.

4. **Pray.** Bring all your spiritual resources to bear. Invite others to pray as well, even the hard-headed business types. You might be surprised. Evangelical churches sometimes talk about "prayer warriors," those who fight the spiritual battle on their knees. If you've got people who are serious about prayer in your church or in your life, invite them to pray about the money. Ask them to pray both for you and the church as a whole.

Leadership Matters

Good leadership accomplishes at least two things in relation to money at church.

Good leaders provide a calm presence when anxiety is high. You can't calm others down, but you can manage yourself, and that makes a difference. Have you ever been at a meeting where you could feel the temperature going up in the room? Then when a key person says calmly, "Here's how I think we can handle this," you can almost hear everyone give a sigh of relief.

That's not to say you have to solve every problem for your congregation. Far from it. However, only the pastor occupies that particular leadership position in a congregation. Position matters. Rev. Larry Matthews, one of my mentors, called it **the "L" position**. When you are the pastor, you have a unique opportunity to influence (not control) the emotional tone of the church and the overall level of anxiety. You do this mainly by focusing on yourself and your own functioning.

How do you know you are leading appropriately? You work on taking the right amount of responsibility, neither overfunctioning nor underfunctioning. As we've discussed earlier, overfunctioners take too much responsibility for others, while underfunctioners don't take enough. Most pastors chronically overfunction, except in money matters. If you feel inadequate in the financial area, you may allow others to take too much of the lead. If you have a financial background, you may find yourself taking too much responsibility in this area, too.

Remember, overfunctioning and underfunctioning are reciprocal. It takes two to tango. If you're carrying too much of the load, someone else is not carrying enough—it's about the relationship. If you're not carrying enough, someone else is taking up the slack (staff or lay leaders). It may be time for you to step it down—or step it up.

Appropriate pastoral responsibility can differ depending on the size and structure of your congregation. Here are some questions to help you discern where you are on this continuum:

1. Am I clear on what my job is and what it isn't in financial matters? Are my lay leaders in agreement about this? Are we clear about mutual responsibilities and accountabilities?

2. Do I remind anyone of their responsibilities in relation to money?

3. Does anyone remind me?

4. Do I lie awake worrying about the money? Does anyone else?

5. Can I read the church financial statements adequately?

6. Am I comfortable asking people to give, or am I at least getting better at it?

I would love to see every pastoral leader talk about money and see it as an important part of their responsibilities. One lay leader said to me, "Our pastor doesn't talk about money, and we don't want him to." They were in agreement, yet I still would question the effectiveness of the agreement.

Relationships Matter

Relationships matter in every area of ministry, of course, but we're talking about money here. Stay connected to the money people. Even if you are not the senior pastor, it pays to keep in touch. Budget conversations will go more smoothly if you have ongoing relationships.

If you are the senior clergy, stay in touch with key lay leaders and staff. The relationships will help carry you through tough times. You don't have to talk about money every time you talk, of course. It's better if you don't. Developing these relationships is like money in the bank (maybe literally at times) that will enhance your leadership. You'll have more credibility with them and others.

As we've seen, one key idea in Bowen family systems theory is emotional triangles. Triangles are one way that relationships commonly play out in financial matters.

Here are some basic ways triangles work:

1. You can't change (for more than a week) a relationship you don't belong to.

2. If you try to change another side of a triangle, the situation often gets worse.

3. When you try to change the relationship of the two others, you carry the stress that belongs to the other two.

4. You *can* change a relationship you belong to because you are part of it. If you change, the relationship changes.[4]

Let's look at a couple of examples:

Pastor-treasurer-congregation president. The treasurer and the president may start having difficulties. Perhaps the reports are late or not adequate. The president complains to the pastor. The president feels better; the pastor feels worse. That's the nature of triangles. The pastor may feel a responsibility to sort out the troubled relationship.

In this case, you as pastor might coach the president to talk to the treasurer directly. You could also work to let go of responsibility for the relationship *and* the reports (easier said than done, I know).

Another example could be **pastor-board-congregation**. The board may want the pastor to preach a bang-up stewardship sermon, so people give and the budget pressure on the board isn't so intense.

What you might do instead: Acknowledge your real responsibility to lead in stewardship. Then keep pushing the responsibility for the budget back to the board. You might even say, "I'm not sure *what* we're going to do about the budget this year." The purpose is not to be truly helpless or to abdicate leadership. It's to make sure some of the anxiety lands where it belongs—on the board, not solely with you.

None of these are quick fixes. However, paying attention to triangles (and actually drawing them out on paper or a board) can help you lower your stress and get clear. You may want to get a coach to help you sort them out when in intense situations. I do this for clergy and get coaching myself to help see the triangles in my work.

History Matters

Your church's history deeply influences the present. We might love to leave the past behind and create a completely new future. However, the past is always present. If you look into the past of your church, you may be surprised how much of that past still goes on in the present.

Here are a few ways history may repeat itself in a congregation's financial challenges and strengths:

- An angel donor who rescues the budget every year.

- Capable financial leaders.

- Periodic conflicts about staff salaries.

- A financial committee or board that always functions well—or never does.

- Strong support for mission and outreach over generations.

What is true about your church? Here are some recommendations:

1. Read the history of the founding of your church. See what you can see. The original DNA is probably still there.

2. Talk with the oldest members of your church. Ask them about previous pastors and leaders and their approach to giving.

3. Talk about money with your predecessors who are still living. One pastor found that every single predecessor told the same story: the pastor got the blame for the financial challenges the congregation was facing.

4. Keep your expectations of how much you can change these deeply rooted patterns in a realistic range. You'll be happier and less frustrated.

5. Take the long view—ideally, an eternal view. The challenges didn't come about in a day or a year. They won't be solved quickly, and that's all right.

6. Celebrate what is right about the past. It's easy for pastors to see what's wrong and what should be changed. Celebrate those who gave, those who built the building, and all the ministry that has been done in that place.

In addition, your own history matters. We all learn the meaning of money in the families we grow up in. I talked at length in the last chapter about getting reflective about your family of origin. Using money as a topic for family exploration can be a valuable contribution to your ministry in this important area.[5]

What Every Pastor Ought to Know About Money

Practically speaking, here are five important things about money every pastor ought to know. Any one of them can be difficult to learn, depending on your background, life experience, and aptitude. However, over time (in some cases, years) and with practice, you'll be better able to lead in stewardship and overall church financial matters.

1. **How to give.** It's hard to teach what you don't know. You may have been raised in a family that was generous, or maybe you weren't.

You may have ample resources, or you may struggle under the weight of a small salary and large debt. Whatever your situation, prayerfully consider how you can be generous and what God is calling you to give.

2. **Your own cash flow.** Figure out how money flows into and out of your life. Make note of your financial priorities. Know whether you are facing a surplus or a deficit each month. Be sure you are making intentional decisions about spending, saving, and giving. This will help with #1. I know people who resist doing this. But I've noticed that not knowing takes more energy than knowing. Facts can calm you down and help you take action, even if the bottom line doesn't look great. If you have a surplus, you can make more intentional choices about how you use the money you do have.

3. **How to read a financial statement.** I didn't learn much about this until I had been a pastor for a number of years. I'll ever be grateful to Andover Newton Theological Seminary, which offered a continuing education seminar on this topic. It transformed my relationship with our financial reports. The teacher understood money AND church and knew how to teach others about it. For the first time I understood what a balance sheet was. I could assess our annual report and even see how to improve it. It boosted my confidence to think that I could make a real contribution to discussions about our reporting. If you don't have a business background, take a course or find a mentor. Experienced pastor Zina Jacques says that pastors "need a coach, someone they can take the budget to and sit with, someone they can ask the basic questions." She suggests pastors find someone for whom "no question is too dumb." She recommends somebody outside the church who can help you read through the reports before a meeting.[6]

4. **How to ask people to give.** You don't have to apologize or feel you're being intrusive. Remember, it's a gift to give people the opportunity to give to causes they believe in. You can work on your learning in a couple of ways. First, you can help people grow in stewardship in their lives as disciples. The second way you can learn to ask people to give is to ask specific people with resources to support special projects. Many pastors never do this. If you have done a capital campaign, you may have had this opportunity. I hated it at first, but I've learned so much by doing it. I have found it a blessing (and still growth-producing) to ask.

5. **That money is a tool.** As I said earlier, we shy away from money talk and from asking for money, as if money were suspect or even dirty. But money, given well, makes ministry possible. The flow of money can be a blessing.

What to Do If There's Not Enough Money

When congregations don't have enough money, anxiety goes up, whether they knew it was coming or not. You've probably experienced a time of financial challenges in your ministry and observed this. Even churches with a substantial endowment experience years when endowment income or giving drops and a budget gap opens.

At times like this, many churches look to the pastor for leadership. This can challenge pastors who are uncomfortable talking about money and really don't know where to start. In some churches, lay leaders want to leave the pastor out, and that's another kind of challenge. Either way, your leadership is essential.

Where to start? This is a chance to put three key leadership practices into practice: **get clear, stay connected, and keep calm**. Remember, every crisis is an opportunity for growth. If you can take it on as an opportunity, you'll do better.

So, first of all, **get clear**. There are two steps to this.

First step: Assess the situation. You'll need to do this with others to get the needed information.

Here are some questions to consider:

1. Is this the result of a long-term decline that has finally moved into crisis territory? What decisions has the leadership made over time as the decline has occurred?

2. Is it a sudden drop? Do you know some of the factors? Always ask, "Why now?" You may not be able to assess all the factors, but it helps get you more neutral and less reactive. Stay in research mode. Note: In a situation like this, you need to know something about the giving patterns of individuals. If you know nothing, it's harder to assess. If the culture of your church is one in which the pastor doesn't know, ask for at least some information. Some possible factors:

- Death or move of a long-time large giver.

- Changes in family circumstances such as divorce or personal financial setbacks.

- Reactivity by one or more givers to a leadership move by you or the board.

3. How serious is it? Do you have enough money to make payroll? Do you have five years of money? And what's the church culture? In some congregations, the members can be in denial about the financial

challenge when there's barely enough for the month. In other churches, a million dollars in cash doesn't seem enough. The facts don't always fit the reaction.

4. What is the congregation's history in facing financial challenges? See how far back you can go with this research. One church took 17 years to become self-supporting, back in the nineteenth century. That history still affects patterns in the congregation, and knowing the past gives perspective on the present.

5. How open is this church with information about money and other matters? Do the leaders keep secrets or share with the congregation?

Second step to getting clear: Determine your thinking. What would you like to say to the leadership about this matter? Remember, you don't have to solve this alone. But you do have the responsibility to say what you think. It's best to figure this out alone.

Do some writing, ideally by hand, about what you think. Try completing one or more of these sentences:

I think . . .

I stand for . . .

I believe . . .

I want . . .

I request . . .

Then, **stay in touch.** Stay connected with key leaders. Look especially for those who are generally calm and have a sense of resourcefulness.

Even if you have financial skills, don't go it alone. Make sure you are partnering with lay leaders, even if you are not sure they are up to it. If your leaders are anxious or not that skilled, work with what you have. Coach them to bring their best thinking to the challenge.

On the other hand, if you have high-functioning (even overfunctioning) leaders who want to keep you out of key conversations, don't let them. Insist on being included.

You can be positive, but don't be a cheerleader. It's exhausting. The most negative people can always outlast you. They can always come up with one more reason why it won't work. Instead, focus on the facts, on your own thinking, and on asking them for their thinking.

When anxiety is high, it can be hard to get facts in some church systems. However, accurate figures, even when they are difficult ones, are less anxiety-producing than not knowing. It's like people who have a lot of credit card debt but don't really know how much. They can calm down when they see the real numbers, know the facts, and can start working toward a repayment plan.

In these conversations, try questions like these:

How have you made it through challenges before?

What's the hardest decision you've ever made as a church?

What resources (not only financial) do we have that will help us
    get through this?

Then ask, **what are the many ways we can solve this problem?** Come up with a lot of possible solutions. Twenty is not too many. Some will not be realistic, but it doesn't matter. There will be one, two, or three decent solutions on the list. You may want to do this for yourself, then with a small group of key leaders rather than with a large group.

Remember that anxious systems can make decisions too quickly or put them off too long. What does your church tend to do: lay off staff quickly? Take another $100,000 from the endowment to put off hard decisions? Or . . . ? All problems have many solutions. You are not responsible for generating the solution, but you are part of it. Be clear to yourself about which decisions you can make or influence, and which ones are out of your hands. Let go of what you can't control.

Next, **stay connected with the congregation.** Work toward openness. When you know what you want to ask of the members, communicate clearly. Expect them to be anxious too. Your goal as a leader is not to protect the congregation. Instead, it is to offer them the challenge of what it means to be a community of faith together. That helps everyone grow.

Keep in touch with staff, too, if you have them. Share as much information as you can appropriately. If you're not sure what's going to happen with staff jobs, be honest about that. Acknowledge that this is tough for them.

Occupy your role with grace and bring your spiritual leadership to the task. You can't simply offer an attitude that "God will provide." Instead, give them a sense that no matter what happens, God is present with you all as you walk through these hard conversations and choices.

Finally, continue to keep (relatively) calm.

In any crisis, if leaders can stay calm, the crisis will be less damaging to the whole system. Keep your wits about you as much as you can and remember this is not your problem to solve alone.

Sometimes you can appropriately push the anxiety back to them: "I'm just not sure what we are going to do about this." You don't have to be the savior. This church is theirs, not yours. And ultimately, it's God's church.

If you and other leaders have to make hard decisions, you will face resistance. Not everyone will be happy. Be prepared for that, and don't take it personally. Coach the other leaders to expect it so they are ready. Whatever the leadership decides, some won't like it. Whether they reduce staff, cut mission giving, or simply ride out what they realistically believe is a temporary downturn, it will upset the balance of things now.

If criticism comes your way, remember that it is not about you personally. Instead, it is coming to you because of the leadership role you occupy. Don't argue with people or defend yourself; simply thank them for their concern.

Staying calm can be a challenge if your salary is on the line and your spouse is panicking. You can do creative thinking on your own or with your spouse: twenty things we could do if my salary were reduced. If you know you have options, even ones that aren't ideal, your anxiety will be lower.

However, I don't recommend you offer to take a pay cut. I think that short-circuits the process wherein lay leaders think together about options. It inappropriately lowers their anxiety and takes the pressure off them to be responsible leaders. That may be one of the solutions, and there may be times when it is the best option. But don't start there. Let them ask for it.

If you take a pay cut, I recommend you negotiate less work as part of it, for yourself and for other staff. If staff time and salary are reduced, you can expect some anger. It may be directed at you. Again, don't take it personally.

Strategies for self-management:

- If you are staying awake at night, notice it and accept it. It won't last forever.

- Pray daily.

- Do something physical daily even if it's just a short walk.

Finally, think back to money challenges and crises in your own family. How were they handled? Did you know about them at the time or not until later? Consider telling someone in your family about the current challenge and asking for their advice. You might be surprised at the wisdom they can provide. Even if they don't, you will probably find yourself less anxious.

Every church has resources and challenges with its resources. Consider what you can celebrate about your congregation, its resources, and the faithful givers who have supported it over the years. Thank God for them—and thank them for what they have done.

Questions for Reflection

How clear are you on where your congregation stands financially?

In what ways might you improve your grasp of finances?

What is your theological understanding of money in the light of faith?

In what ways does your anxiety manifest itself when money
  issues come up?

In what ways are you taking leadership in stewardship and
  finance? What else might you try?

How are you relating to key financial and other leaders?

How much do you know about the history of your church and its
  finances? How might you find out more?

6

Communication

Can You Get Free of Needing People to Agree?

Let your conversation be always full of grace, seasoned with salt, so that you may know how to answer everyone.

—COL. 4:6 (NRSV)

I came across a quote recently in a decades-old letter by Murray Bowen. He said, "The more I can define me, the more I can respect the others . . ."[1] I realized how often I don't truly listen to and respect others who have a different perspective. I just want them to agree with me.

In ministry, we spend a lot of energy on the content and technique of communication, from the practice of preaching to the social media platform of the moment. However, the best technique will fail if you don't attend to the crucial element of relationships.

Communication Requires Relationship

Communication is rooted in relationships. How and whether people hear you depend on what kind of relationship they have with you. This is true even in larger churches where not everyone may know you personally. It's true when a parent speaks to a child and when a president addresses the nation.

Rabbi Edwin Friedman talked about this emotional side of communication. His counsel has been more helpful to me than any other communication training I've had.

Friedman talked about what he called "three inter-relational variables":

1. Direction

2. Distance

3. Anxiety

If you pay attention to these variables, you will almost automatically communicate better AND be less frustrated. Let's talk about each one.

Direction

"Others can only hear you when they are moving toward you, no matter how eloquently you phrase the message. In other words, when you are in a pursuing, rescuing, or coercive position, your message, no matter how eloquently broadcast, will never catch up."

—Edwin Friedman[2]

When you try to communicate with others, pay attention to what direction they are moving. Are they coming toward you, emotionally speaking, or moving away?

When my kids were growing up, if I said, "Clean your room!" they were never moving toward me. If I said, "Ice cream!" they could hear me wherever they were in the house (and we lived in a large church parsonage).

Over time, you can get better at assessing the direction people are moving. However, I imagine you could already do a pretty good job of knowing who among your key leaders is moving toward you and who is moving away.

A close to surefire tip: do their eyes light up? Or do they glaze over? Typically, when someone's eyes glaze over, we keep talking. We think if we marshal better arguments they will come around. Instead, I recommend you STOP pursuing people who aren't getting the message. Instead, **connect**. Stay in touch, without trying to persuade. Be patient—it may take months or even years for some folks.

Assessing the direction people are moving in will give you a different perspective. You will be less inclined to try to talk an individual or a group into something—which rarely is effective in the long term. You will spend more time talking to those who are motivated and simply relating to those who aren't.

It's easy to get impatient when our message is important:

- *God is calling us to a new ministry with people in need in our community!*

- *We will be in serious financial trouble if we don't make some changes now!*

- *Our worship isn't connecting with our younger or newer people!*

- *We can't just go back to the way things were in the past. We have to move forward!*

However, if people aren't coming toward you, you are wasting your words. Stop talking, take a deep breath, and look around for those whose eyes light up. Talk to them. They are ready to hear your message. Over time you can experiment and see if others are ready to hear.

Distance

"People who are too far or too close can't hear each other."

—Edwin Friedman[3]

When you set out to deliver a message, assess how close or far the person is emotionally. You may have trouble communicating if the person is *either* too close to you or too far from you.

Too close: if there's no emotional space, there's no room to communicate.

The classic examples are parents and teenagers, and spouses with each other. A parent can try like crazy to communicate the value of education with no response. Then the kid comes home quoting the same message from a friend's parent. The parent thinks, "I've been saying that for months—how did she get through to this kid?" There's more emotional space with the friend's parent, and so, more ability to hear the message. Likewise, a spouse may start exercising on the advice of a colleague when you have been talking to a brick wall for years.

At church, this might show up in the finance committee when the chair can't hear what the senior pastor is saying but can hear it from a calm person on the committee. Or the youth pastor can hear what a youth group member says when he can't hear the same message from his own son.

Too far: if you aren't well enough connected with people, they won't be able to hear you. There's not enough of a relationship. They are too far from you emotionally.

When you first enter a congregation, as you no doubt know, it takes time to get established. Make sure you take this into account when communicating. Listening is a higher priority than speaking at this stage. When you truly listen to someone, the likelihood is that they will move closer to you.

Over time, you can move closer to people who may be at a distance. The trick is to do this without pursuing them. When people know you are not trying to change or convert them, they are less likely to stay distant. That said, you know there are always some in the congregation who stay at a distance. Others may move closer or farther away over time.

Once, when I interviewed for a pastoral position, this showed up quite literally in physical position. A search committee member told me that years previously he had strongly disagreed with the choice of a new pastor. He kept coming to worship but sat in the balcony, which was far, far from the pulpit. Over time, he moved back down to his usual pew. I'm sure that after that move the pastor was more able to communicate with him.

Anxiety

"As for anxiety, it is the static in any communication system and can distort or scramble any message. It cannot be eliminated simply by turning up the volume, since that invariably also turns up the static."

—Edwin Friedman[4]

When people go to the doctor, they can find it hard to remember what the doctor says. It's not just the medical jargon: their anxiety is higher, and they find it harder to process the information.

When anxiety in a congregation goes up, communication will be more difficult. Anxiety *is* like static. People simply can't hear as easily. In a time of major transition, during pre- and post-sabbatical weeks, or when there's a big conflict, pay even more attention to communication than usual. Don't be surprised if people act like they haven't heard a message. They haven't.

While communication strategy is important, it's about more than strategy. You may need to get the message out more frequently, but you can't simply get louder. Simply trying harder to help people get it can be counterproductive.

You need to keep the big picture in mind. Ask yourself:

What is going on in the church as a whole?

- Are there larger issues (community, denominational) which may be raising people's anxiety?

- What is the history of the church with this particular issue?

Most important of all, work on managing your own anxiety. You can't lower the anxiety in a system without regulating the anxiety YOU are putting into it. I've heard that Murray Bowen used to say, "You only need to be the least anxious person in the room." In some rooms, it's not that hard.

The Other Side of Communication: Listening

Susan Scott, in *Fierce Conversations*, writes, "Do you know someone who will most likely die with his or her mouth open? Many CEOs I know would make this list. That is not good. A dazzling way with words rarely proves to be enough to guarantee success as a leader." [5] Many pastors would also make the list. We're preachers, after all.

Every pastor needs two critical communication skills: speaking and listening. The delivery side is important. I mentioned earlier Bowen's quote, "The more I define me, the more I can respect the others." But here I'm going to talk about that second piece of communication. Respecting the others includes listening or receiving their messages. Notice that silence is mentioned first in Eccl. 3:7: "a time to keep silence" *then* "a time to speak."

Why Truly Listening Is Important

First, listening is important for its own sake. People deserve to be listened to. In fact, no ministry action may be more powerful than listening. Yet most people don't know how to do it well. Consequently, most people almost never encounter a real listener. What could be a better gift to give them?

Second, listening can help your leadership. When you truly listen to people, without immediately trying to convince them of something, they are more likely to listen to you when you do speak. You will have a stronger relationship with them. Listening is like capital in the bank for future leadership endeavors.

Discern What You Are Doing

Are you truly listening? Pay attention to what you are doing in the moment when someone is talking to you. Whether you are listening to your assistant, a parishioner, or one of your children, you may realize you are not listening. If you are thinking about the topic, you may realize you are thinking about what you are going to say next. Or you may be thinking about what you have to do after the conversation is over.

Some years ago, I went to a workshop where communication was a topic. We had "communication homework": Go home and listen to someone in our family for three minutes. So, I told my husband, "I've got homework tonight." I listened to him for the assigned time. Then I said, "I realized I don't listen to you very well." He said, "I know." That was a moment of truth. We'd been married for over 30 years. I do a lot of listening to clergy and others in the work I do. However, I wasn't listening well at all to the person I'm closest to. I've worked to get better at it. For one thing, I don't fold the laundry when he's talking to me anymore. I try not to think about the next thing I'm going to do or how I'm going to respond. I also remember with gratitude how well he's listened to me all these years.

Listening can become a spiritual practice. We can take these few minutes to be with someone who is a child of God. Whether we like what they say or don't, agree or disagree, are engaged or bored, we can stay in the moment.

Here are some elements of true listening:

- Paying attention to the other

- Letting go of thoughts about what you will say next.

- Letting go of judgmental thoughts about what they are saying.

- Giving them time to finish.

Manage Your Anxiety While You Are Listening

It's easy to get anxious when people are talking to you. They may be criticizing you or someone else in the congregation. They may want some advice that you're not sure how to give. What they say may trigger something deep in you from your family of origin. They may be creating a triangle that hooks you. ("Pastor, you've really got do something about Mary . . .") You may simply be worried about how much more time this will take.

Here are a few ideas when you feel your anxiety rising:

- Breathe.

- Stay in the moment.

- Let go of the need to fix anything or the invitation into the triangle. "Feel the back of your chair," as a coach of mine once recommended.

- Pray for the one you are listening to.

- Ask questions for clarification.

Remember, this is one of the most challenging parts of ministry. If you walk away from a conversation feeling anxious, wishing you had responded differently, be kind to yourself. None of us can get it right every time. You'll get another chance to practice tomorrow—perhaps with the same person.

If people calmly and clearly disagree with you, it can be as good for the life of the church as if they enthusiastically sign up. In fact, it's better than unquestioning agreement, which can break down under stress. Learning what they think and why is an important part of leadership.

Listen Without Giving Advice

Don't just listen so you can give them good advice. In fact, don't give advice. Advice is overrated. It's overfunctioning—doing for others what they can do for themselves. People rarely take advice. If they do take it and it doesn't work out, they'll be upset—with you.

Clergy can feel pressure to convince people of something or solve their problems for them. "Isn't that my job?" you may ask. In fact, no. Instead, your job is to be present with others in a way that helps them figure things out for themselves. No one knows what is best for someone else's life. They may come up with a much better idea than you do. And even if it's not as good an idea, the fact that it was their own will make them more likely to implement it.

When You Can't Listen Anymore, Stop

I find pastors may think that they have to listen as long as the other wants to talk, unless they have another appointment and have to leave. It's not true. When you bring your best to listening, there will come a point when you just can't listen anymore. Then it's better to acknowledge that and come back later.

Try saying something like this: "I'm happy to talk about this again later. But I can't give you my full attention anymore, and I want to do that when we talk." If you can't manage that, try: "I have another commitment in about ten minutes" (even if the commitment is to yourself).

I've been there as a pastor. I know some people barely draw breath, so you can't even break in. It's all right to interrupt them. For unregulated people, setting time boundaries is doing them a favor— as well as yourself. In the moment, it can be difficult. It feels mean to cut someone off. But you don't have time to talk to everyone who wants to talk to you for as long as they want to. If you do, you can't carry out the work of leadership.

In ministry, I found that in pastoral care, I could spend less time with people and still do good listening. Sometimes I would plan in advance: I'm not going to stay longer than 45 minutes. There's a good reason therapy sessions are 50 minutes. It's hard to listen longer than that, so you aren't doing much good when a conversation goes longer. In the ministry, you don't have the structure that therapists do, so you have to set limits yourself.

What are the benefits of truly listening?

- It enhances your presence with individuals and as a leader.

- People will be more able to hear you when they know you will, in turn, listen to them.

- It helps in conflict. If people sense that you are truly listening to them, not just trying to persuade them of your point of view, they will calm down.[6] Edwin Friedman used to say, "Leadership is not about technique but about the nature of your presence." Listening can be used as a technique, but if you are truly present with people as you listen, something can shift in the relationship.

True listening has benefits beyond the church. Imagine if you truly listened to your spouse, your teenager, or your mother. Listening is a practice you can do every day, everywhere.

The most important listening of all is listening to God. I'll say more about this later.

Speaking So That People Will Listen

Now I want to speak about another aspect of communication: speaking so people will listen. This is a hard lesson for preachers to learn. It can be almost as hard for us as listening to others. We are so convinced of the rightness of our message that we think if we just say it, people will get it. Here are five ways to improve your "listenability" in any setting from the pulpit to a board meeting to individual conversations.

1. **Be clear.** Define yourself. If you have time to prepare, think through your own principles and beliefs and how they apply to this situation. I often say the best example of this that I know is Martin Luther King's "I Have a Dream" speech.[7] A more recent example is the statement Rick Warren made to the Southern Baptist Convention about Baptist identity and principles. He wrote an open letter in

response to the ever-increasing growing creedalism and theological rigidity of Southern Baptists. He said, "Hand me a Bible and I'll sign *that* as my authority. The Bible is Baptist's [*sic*] *sole* authority."[8]

Murray Bowen said this about family life: "When one member of a family can calmly state his own convictions and beliefs, and take action on his convictions without criticism of the beliefs of others and without becoming involved in emotional debate, then other family members will start the same process of becoming more sure of self and more accepting of others."[9]

2. **Be discerning.** You don't need to tell them *everything* you are thinking right now. The art of leadership includes discerning when to be upfront and when to keep your own counsel. In general, I think greater openness is better than less. At the same time, it's critical to assess what people are ready to hear and to time the pacing of your message over time.

Pay attention to:

- The length of your tenure in the congregation.

- The overall level of anxiety.

- The maturity level of the group you are addressing.

- The level of change your message advocates. (The more disruptive the change, the more you need to space the message out over time.)

3. **Speak for yourself.** Practice using the pronoun "I." Avoid "you," especially as in "you ought" or "you should." Again, King in his I Have a Dream speech doesn't say "you" or "we." He simply shares a vivid description of what his dream is.

In addition, don't speak for others: "Sally thinks." Allow people to speak for themselves.

Pay attention to your listeners, whether in conversation, meetings, or worship. If their eyes are glazing over or they are getting restless, it's time to stop. Leave them wanting more.

4. **Be open to feedback.** This doesn't mean you necessarily will do what someone else wants you to do, but you may need to adjust direction based on the feedback they give. Instead of explaining yourself further, invite them to say more about their perspective.

5. **Don't try to convince others.** You are inviting and enrolling others, not trying to talk them into anything. You don't want them to say yes unless it's a real yes. The results will not be good for anyone if they say yes because they feel coerced. They usually end up acting like they said no.

You could consider telling people to say "no" to you unless they plan to stand by their yes. The online shoe company Zappos offered people who went through their training program $2,000 at the end if they left. Tony Hsieh, the CEO, only wanted people who were really committed.[10]

Most of these recommendations can be used in any setting: individual conversations, board meetings, congregational meetings, or from the pulpit. Of course, you don't always have a chance to prepare. If someone catches you on the fly, do your best to follow them. Focus on your own best thinking in the moment, and feel free to say, "I'd like to think about this a little more." Then go home and do the hard work of thinking it through and have a further conversation.

Your presence may be a clear form of communication in itself. Ron Richardson in *Polarization and the Healthier Church* talks about a polarized racial conversation he was in many years ago. He says of one group: "I was not sufficiently connected to them to make open 'I' position statements. . . . My 'I' position was evident in how I was present with them and how I related to them, rather than through openly stating my beliefs, and that is what worked."[11] Showing up can speak volumes.

Planning Ahead: Why, What, How, and When

There are plenty of communication opportunities when you can plan ahead: sermons, speaking to board meetings and other groups, email, snail mail, and social media. While communication is more about relationships than technique, technique does matter. Here are some practical ideas:

Know Why

Get clear about your purpose for each communication and each medium/platform. Write it out. One sentence is plenty. It doesn't have to be profound, just clear. "The purpose for _______ is."

Examples:

"My purpose for preaching this quarter is to help people to connect their spiritual life with a call to act in the world."

"The purpose of this sermon is to help people experience God's grace."

"The purpose of this letter is to motivate our members and friends to complete and send in their pledges for next year."

"My/our purpose for using [any social media platform] is to create an ongoing conversation about faith and daily life."

"My purpose for this post is to encourage engagement by means of a thoughtful question."

"The purpose of this email is to invite board members to pray before the budget discussion next Tuesday."

Know What

Finding content is an ongoing task for all communicators. A system for planning ahead and collecting and accessing ideas will save you hours. One pastor has been using a box of 3×5 cards to collect ideas since he was ten years old and saw the box his own pastor used. That can still work! I have an ongoing Google Docs list of ideas, where I try to add one idea a day for my newsletter and other articles. Note: it doesn't have to be a good idea. Keep collecting ideas, and some of them will be good. If you know what at least your next few sermons will be, you can scout for illustrations.

Know How

Sometimes it's obvious what medium to use for communication. The annual report to the congregation will likely be in written form and may have a verbal component at the annual meeting. Sometimes you may want to consult others. For example, "What's the best way to get our stewardship message out this year?" You may use a combination of in-person communication from the pulpit and from lay leaders, video, email, and snail mail. Keep your purpose in mind as you create the plan. It might be, as I mentioned above, "To motivate our members and friends to complete and send in their pledges for next year." Or, it could be, "To encourage members and friends to thoughtfully consider percentage giving next year." The purpose may affect how you choose to deliver the message.[12]

Know When

Whatever the message is and whatever the platform, when will it go out? How long do you need to prepare for it and when will it happen? You need more lead time in a larger congregation, especially if others are involved. Leave time for the planning and the message to germinate.

Clergy differ widely in how and when they manage sermon prep time. I knew one pastor who always wrote her sermon at 5:30 a.m. on Sunday. That would have put me in an early grave. However, it worked for her. Know yourself and how you work best.

One more note on when: If you're speaking, from the pulpit or elsewhere: **know when to stop.** Have a clear sense of how long you want to speak and stick to it. Leave them wanting more. It's no secret that attention spans are getting shorter. Don't give a monologue. Give people time to reflect. One brilliant teacher I had rarely spoke for more than seven or eight minutes. He then offered time to think. You can even do this in a sermon: I recently heard a preacher who began with a moment of silence, then stopped in the middle and invited people to another moment of silence before he continued. Some highly skilled preachers can hold a congregation for 45 minutes, but that's not me, and it's probably not you.

What Did You Learn from Your Family About Communication?

Finally, I want to return to the emotional aspects of communication. We all learn how to communicate in the families in which we grow up. We learn our first words. We learn how to listen. We spend years watching others communicate.

Then we go into ministry, where communication is essential. We relate to members and families who also grew up in families where they learned how to communicate, often in ways different from ours. What's more, the congregation has its own history and patterns of communication.

Anxiety and Communication

Chronic anxiety deeply affects communication. It can manifest in family communication patterns in ways like these:

- Conflict: communication through fighting

- Distancing: communicating via silence or secrets

- Pursuit: someone persistently trying to get a message across to another (often "for their own good"), who emotionally distances in return—or physically distances by moving away

It's not just about the immediate family experience. Families have multigenerational processes at work. Consider what you already know about your extended family over the generations: Who talked to whom? Who was left out? Who fought with whom, and what was the story about that?

Many families have secrets and keep silence around them. What was never discussed in your family? In my own family, there was a big secret about a family tragedy in my father's family. When his mother was 18, her father killed her mother, and then killed himself. My grandmother never talked about it. My grandfather told my father when he was a young adult. Dad told my brother and me about it when we were young adults (right before I got married, in fact).

The power of this secret was such that I forgot about it. My father told me again when I was in my thirties, and I was then at a place in my life where I could reflect more thoughtfully on the event, the secret, and its impact on my father—and on me.

My aversion to conflict has deep roots. It's multigenerational. Talking about difficult subjects where people might get angry takes a lot of energy for me. I'm better at it than I used to be, but it's not my greatest strength.

In my mother's family, people talked about ideas and people, but not about feelings. We're all very nice, not very critical. As my mother aged, I noticed she could be a know-it-all. (I can, too, under stress.) But she was nice about it. My first response if I say something that might be "not nice" is to feel guilty about it. Honest communication about difficult topics is not natural on either side of my family.

Take time to reflect on the relationships and communication patterns in your family. It's not easy. A coach can assist you with this work. It's taken me years to sort through some matters. But even a surface reflection can help you gain more insight into what you do.

Communication Strengths

It's always easy to focus on the challenges in our families, but remember the strengths as well.

Both of my parents loved people. One of their highest compliments was "He's a people person." Until the end of his life, my father would engage with anyone he saw. He was in sales, making calls on prospects daily, and loved it. He never met a stranger. My mother always made conversation with store clerks and was the first to greet visitors at church. While I'm not an extrovert, I also can talk to just about anyone. It's an asset in ministry. I'm grateful for the gifts I received from my family.

Other families have different strengths:

- Fighting and making up in a loving way.

- Being quiet together.

- Being candid without belittling.

- Giving advice without willfulness.

Even if your family communicated in ways that were challenging for you, they may have offered you gifts for ministry. I've coached more than one pastor who grew up in a high-conflict family and ended up in a high-conflict congregation. Their youthful experience, difficult as it was, served them well in teaching them how to lead in a tough setting. They know how to get in people's faces productively in a way I will never learn.

What communication gifts did your family give you?

Navigating Different Communication Styles

Almost every family has some cross-cultural elements: Two families join and bring their different approaches to communication. You've probably experienced navigating those differences. Visiting your mother's family was different from visiting your father's. If you didn't see extended family, you observed the interaction between your parents—or whoever raised you—and internalized some of the differences. That can be an asset in itself.

When you sit around a table at a church meeting, bring those lessons to bear. Observe how others communicate. Remember each one has their own family story, which contributes to whether they talk a lot, clam up when things get difficult, try to make peace, or keep information to themselves.

Developing a Wider Repertoire

Whatever you learned from your family, it probably wasn't enough. Ministry requires a repertoire of responses. None of us learned everything we need to communicate at church.

You can practice in a variety of ways. **First,** become more aware of what you do.

Do you:

- Talk more than others? Talk less than others?

- Avoid difficult topics? Launch right in?

- Talk to people? Talk about them?

- Get angry out loud? Get angry silently?

- What else do you notice?

Second, experiment with making different choices.

If you're a talker, talk less in meetings and pastoral care conversations. Even if you know the answer, keep it quiet, for now.

If you tend to be quiet, speak up more. Speak your mind even if you think someone else won't like it. If this is tough for you, start small. (Remember, the color of the carpet in the church isn't a small matter . . .)

It's complicated. In my own case, I need to both shut up more and speak up more, depending. I have to shut up when I could seem to be a know-it-all and speak up even if I think there might be conflict.

Third (advanced), experiment with making different choices **in your family.**

On a family visit, try changing the usual script.

Here are a few ideas:

- If your family isn't interested in church and you never talk about it, try a brief monologue about your ministry.

- If your mother talks on and on about her ailments, instead of tuning out, listen carefully and ask questions.

- If you just go along with what everyone wants to do, say what you want to do.

- If you argue with your father about politics or religion, change the subject. Talk about something lighthearted.

Developing your interpersonal communication is the work of a lifetime. You get the opportunity to practice every day. Each conversation with a church member or staff person and each board meeting is yet another chance to learn about yourself and about them.

In addition, every time you interact with a family member, you can learn more about the forces that shaped you and can experiment with new ways of communicating.

You will have days when you walk away from an encounter kicking yourself, wishing you had said this or hadn't said that. Use those moments to show compassion to yourself. Reflect on what you want to do next time, without judgment, and how you can continue to grow in your communication repertoire.

Questions for Reflection

What's a message you want to share now? To whom do you want to communicate it? Who will be motivated to hear it? Who likely won't?

Try this: Take that message and ask: What's the purpose? What's the best medium? When do I want to share it? When do I want to prepare to do that?

What are your strengths as a listener? How can you become a better listener? To whom do you want to listen better?

What do you notice about communication in your immediate and extended family? What did you learn? How do you live those things out in your ministry? What new approaches might you try?

7

Get Focused

What Do You Want to Do Most?

For everything there is a season, and a time for every matter under heaven.

—(ECCL. 3:1, NRSV)

Anne Lamott says, "It will take time. Time takes time. I hate this."[1] Ministry takes time—time on the clock and time on the calendar. It involves doing and then waiting—then doing some more. Both doing and waiting are hard work. The time factor in ministry is not just about time management. Managing *self* in relation to the work and the waiting is a critical skill for ministry. That includes knowing how *you* work best. I share here approaches to priorities, focus, and time boundaries. Experiment to see what works for you.

What's Most Important Now

You may find yourself working too hard without ever being clear about what is most important to you. Other people will be happy to tell you what's important: "Pastor, I think you should . . ."

It's critical to take the time periodically to think through your *own* priorities. It's a differentiating exercise in leadership. What do you want to do in your work at this time? What makes sense, given the responsibilities of your role?

If you set intentional priorities, you can make your life easier and your ministry more effective. You can make decisions more quickly, get started at work faster each day, and get home earlier. Priorities create a boundary between what you will do and won't do, at least for now.

Decide on Your Priorities

Here are ways to work on discerning priorities:

Prayer. Prayerfully consider what makes sense for you: *What does God want me to do this year, this quarter, this week, this day?* It's an ongoing, prayerful, reflective process. A personal planning retreat is one way to take a chunk of time for this work. Or you could use your daily prayer time for discernment over several days.

Desire. What do you *want* your priorities to be? What sounds like fun? What do you want to do in ministry and your personal life? God speaks to us through our desires more often than we think. Does your heart leap when you pray or think about an item? Consider moving it higher on your list. If more clergy found more joy in ministry, both they and their congregations would benefit.

Necessity. Every job includes things you simply have to do, whether you are in the mood or not. If you are the preacher, you have to write the sermon. Some of the tasks just go with the job, like preaching, worship planning, paying attention to the finances, and staff supervision. You have to do a certain amount of pastoral visitation, especially in crisis. However, overfunctioning clergy often think they have to do more than is really necessary.

I recommend that you take on only one or two new projects beyond your routine ministry. You can't have fifteen priorities, especially if you are trying to start something new. Be realistic about what you can actually achieve in the time you have. I truly believe we have enough time to do everything God wants us to do.

Use Your Priorities to Help You Plan

Once you have discerned what is most important to do, you can use your thinking to help you plan. Look ahead at your week. This may seem obvious. Yet I'm shocked at how many weeks I simply dived right in without looking at more than my appointments. Instead, ask yourself in advance: *How many hours do I want to work this week, and when?* You can do this at the end of each week or the beginning of the next one.

Then ask: *When am I going to work on my highest priority items?* If you block out the time, you are less likely to give it away to something less important. You can always tell someone, "I have an appointment at that time." It will be true: You have an appointment with yourself.

Include personal time in your planning. What time will you take off? What evenings will you be home? Block the time out so you don't fill it up with work or additional meetings. That's an appointment with yourself, too.

Plan to work on your most important projects in your highest energy time. For me, it's morning. I know there's no point in trying to write something original in the late afternoon. My brain simply quits working. I know other people, including my son and daughter, who just get started with their creative work later in the day.

At the beginning of every day, or the end of the day before, review your plan. Rev. Mindi Welton-Mitchell says she sets only one to three intentions for the day to help her stay focused. She also suggests leaving some margin in between appointments (and before and after vacation).[2]

Map out your time as best as you can predict. If you have a set time to work on something (and to stop working on it), you'll be able to work faster. A deadline creates pressure to produce.

My salesman father always had a pocket calendar that said on the cover, "Plan your work and work your plan." I wish I'd learned that lesson a lot earlier.

Use Your Priorities to Help You Say No

The way to an overwhelmed schedule is to say yes to great ideas that are not true priorities for you. I talk to a lot of clergy who have a hard time saying no. If it's a good idea, or a request from someone they like or respect, they want to say yes. They do and end up over their heads.

Just because it's a good idea doesn't mean you should say yes. To make progress, you can't take on too much. I've learned the hard way that that is the way to frustration. You have too many projects you never complete. You get overwhelmed because the deadlines come at once. Or you have back-to-back meetings day after day. You can't make your best contribution when you are juggling too many commitments.

Before you say yes to anything, say, "Let me think about it and get back to you." Make it a personal policy not to say yes right away.

Then ask yourself:

- Does this fit with my current priorities and plan?

- Do I sense a call to this?

- Do I want to?

- Do I have time?

Don't say yes unless you can answer yes to at least three of these questions. One exception may be a key player's pet project that you consider for strategic reasons. You may want to say yes to a request from the bishop or a congregation power broker, for example. But don't do this too often. Don't be afraid to say no at times, even to the bishop or other key leaders. It may garner you respect.

Consider partnering with a friend or colleague for mutual discernment about these opportunities. A partner may make it easier to say no. A mentor or spiritual director may also be helpful in this.

Adjust as Needed

You can unexpectedly find that you need to change your ministry priorities. It took place on a huge scale in March 2020 when churches had to shut down in-person worship. This happens in smaller ways all the time. An unexpected death in the congregation changes your weekly plan immediately. A staff resignation, an upset church member, or simply a broken copier may require your attention. Some weeks you may feel like your entire plan has gone haywire.

One approach: Take weeks like this as an opportunity for spiritual practice. Rather than gritting your teeth with frustration, practice acceptance. Breathe. Pray. Take a few moments to gather your thoughts. You can ask yourself, "Given this, what are my priorities for today?" Or "How can I get through this week with grace?"

Week to week, the routine tasks and small crises of ministry easily crowd out the ministry initiatives that you want to move forward. Some weeks you will have no time for those larger efforts at all. I want to normalize this, so you don't get too frustrated. I also want to challenge you to do your best to schedule time most weeks for the higher priorities.

Remember that part of the resistance to change in congregations is this: low-level crises can appear. When you move forward, you upset the balance of your congregation. You push one part of a mobile, and another part starts to bounce. You make a big change in worship and your admin starts to act out. Or there's a problem in the children's ministry. Yes, you must give your attention to the mobile's "bounce." But don't let it distract you too much from your general direction and higher priorities. If you don't have an hour for a big-picture goal, give it 15 minutes. You'll make progress little by little.

Evaluate and Assess

Periodically (quarterly and annually), review your priorities and see where you are with them. Life changes, and implementation brings feedback that may cause you to make some changes. This happened to me while writing this book. I had a different concept for it. Some key feedback made me realize that it would not be the book I wanted. I had to change my approach, which meant (sigh) starting over.

Even if you do say yes, it's not a lifetime commitment. You can change your mind: "I've given this some thought, and I just can't keep doing this."

How to Focus

One of the best ways to increase your productivity is to increase your ability to focus day to day and minute to minute. If you can do this, you will get more done, be less stressed, and have more impact in your ministry. It's not easy, though. It's countercultural.

In order to become more focused, you need to solve **two key problems.**

Problem 1: Other People Interrupt You

If you're in the office, you can be interrupted by staff, church members dropping by, calls and texts, emails, and other notifications.

You start to work on something, and you get interrupted. Then you go back to work and have to pick up where you left off. It takes twice as long to finish it. You stay late or work on your day off to finish the sermon. At the end of the day, you think, "What did I get done today?"

To find more focus, you need to develop a strategy for dealing with interruptions. Try these:

Set times when you are not available. Someone said to me once, "If you wouldn't call 911, don't call me." I was a little shocked, but I got the message. If limiting your availability creates a big change for you and your church, keep it small. Start with an hour a day, or even 30 minutes. Tell your assistant, if you have one. Don't answer calls or texts. If you need to, get out of the office. Go to the library or a café. Remember: pastors have not always been constantly available. Many pastors now are not. You can do your job without responding instantly.

To deal with electronic interruptions, turn off notifications. If you get a "ping" every time you get an email or social media response, you will have a hard time focusing.

And: **accept that interruptions are a part of ministry.** Much ministry can take place in the conversations that result from interruptions. In addition, you can't schedule pastoral emergencies. Things simply happen. It's important to be available as a pastor. People need to sense that you are connected to them. You don't want them to see you as aloof or avoiding them.

Any solution that can help you increase focus needs to take this into account. However, if you are constantly available, you will be much less productive. You will do more last-minute planning and work. You will have more trouble taking time off. You will, ironically, have *less* ability to be present with people when they really need you.

Problem 2: You Interrupt Yourself

An even bigger problem: you interrupt your own focus. You start to work on something, and it gets difficult. You're not sure what to do with the scripture text for the week. You decide to take a break and look for a sermon illustration online. You get taken down the rabbit hole of one link leading to another. Thirty minutes later, you finally pull yourself back to work on the sermon itself.

Or you have a knotty congregational issue you need to think through. You take a few notes. Then the idea of having the necessary difficult conversations makes you anxious. You take a social media break and see something from a parishioner that you think you need to respond to. You follow a few headline links. An hour later, you decide you'll think about the original problem tomorrow.

Try this:

Work to create one or two small habits to increase your concentration. For example, check your favorite social media platform only at the beginning and end of the day. Don't try to do too much at once.

Set specific times for checking email. I read somewhere that CEOs don't "check" email, they "process" it at set times. They don't have time to respond as emails come in. Neither do you. I still have to work on this. Be compassionate with yourself and your own addictive tendencies.

Use a timer. If you are working on something hard, set a timer for 20 minutes. Then take a 10-minute break. Or work 45 minutes and take a 15-minute break. I learned this from my daughter when she was studying for her graduate school exams. It really works. I do some variation of this most days during times I don't have appointments. Make sure you take the break when the timer goes off.

Block out a full day to work on one thing. It could be sermon preparation and planning, strategic thinking about ministry, or a personal retreat day to think about your life. If you can do it in the office, God bless you. Most people will need to at least be at home if not someplace completely different. The more you do this, the better you will get at it.

Why Is Focus So Important?

First of all, leadership requires focus. You need to step away from the swirling currents of anxiety to think through what you want in your ministry. You need to think about your leadership and where you sense God calling you and your people next. You need time and space not just once, but on an ongoing basis.

Second, if pastors never think deeply about Scripture, their sermons and teaching will be shallow. They will be scouring the internet for exegesis and sermon illustrations. I know there are wonderful resources online. I preached every week for over 13 years and know how challenging it can be to generate material. Some weeks I was happy simply to have something, anything, to fill that pulpit time. However, there is no long-term substitute for your own thinking. Over time, your people need your best.

Third, if you are constantly distracted, *everything* will take longer. You will have a harder time getting off to be with family or for hobbies (yes, hobbies!).

But I'm an extrovert! Some pastors find it hard to be alone. You do your best thinking in conversation. I'm the daughter of an off-the-charts extrovert, so I know the territory. My dad hated being alone. I'm right in the middle, myself. And I'm married to an off-the-charts introvert, a librarian who worked with the public for years. I know the full spectrum well. The pastors I've coached over the years cover the spectrum, too.

Much of ministry involves spending time with people. Yet knowing your own thinking and generating ideas are also a critical part of ministry. Some thinking develops in conversation, especially for extroverts. However, even for extroverts, the discipline of setting aside time alone to think for yourself is essential.

But I'm an introvert! Introverted pastors have to discipline themselves to get out and make connections. If you do your best work alone, you need lots of time to yourself. Much of ministry involves doing thoughtful reflection, sermon preparation, and planning. However, connecting with people is also essential. If you're an introvert and get tired or anxious, you may avoid people when you need to connect with them.

Whatever your personality, I recommend you make intentional choices. NOW I'm going to hole up and focus. NOW I'm going to connect with folks. If you are not intentional about your time, others will create your schedule for you. One of the blessings of ministry is having far more control over your time than many other people. Use it!

A little improvement will go a long way. What I want for you and for me is freedom—from the trivial, from addictive behaviors that don't serve ourselves, the church, or God's purposes in the world, and from our tendency to do easy things first.

Productivity Can Be Overrated

I'm all for productivity, and for using time effectively. However, being productive can be overrated. Here are a few of those times:

1. **When doing overrides being.** We can be so focused on getting things done that we don't take time to sit, to play, or to be creative. It's easy to fall into this because it is the default position of our culture. Busyness is a value in itself. We feel that the busier we are, the more valuable, productive, and important we are.

Busyness does not equal productivity, as I've said before. Even if you are using your time well, I hope you are also taking time to stop and simply *be*. The temptation is, I'm getting so much done, if I keep going a little longer, I can do even more. Or I can do even more *for God*. (That's a seductive thought.)

Taking time for being can feel lazy. Even if you want to spend more time in prayer and reflection, it feels "unproductive." If you want to take time to do something that feeds your soul that isn't explicitly spiritual, you may feel guilty or selfish.

Remember, God wants you to be yourself, your best self, in ministry and in life. That means you must spend time with yourself, to get to know yourself better, and do the things that help you be yourself most fully. That means occasionally letting go of the need to get things done.

My husband, Karl, is really good at this. Years ago, we lived in an apartment in Berkeley that overlooked our neighbor's lovely garden. One day when I came home, he was looking out the window at the sprinkler going back and forth in the garden. The sun was shining and the water drops sparkled. I asked, "How long have you been sitting there?"

He said, "Oh, about 15 minutes." I was stunned. I'm not sure I've ever stared out the window for 15 minutes at a time. It's something to aspire to. On the other hand, it's easy for me to sit and read a novel for 15 minutes (or more). I do it every single day.

I recommend you do something each day that feeds you, for at least 15 minutes.

2. **When doing overrides being present.** You have your plan laid out. The week is packed. Then someone stops by to chat. Or you get a text about a pastoral emergency. Or you need to deal with a staff or building problem. You want to roll your eyes.

We've discussed interruptions as a part of ministry. There's a time to set aside the plan and simply be present with people. If you are frustrated or impatient, you won't show up with them in the same way.

Remember, you don't have to talk with people as long as they want to talk. You don't want to allow certain individuals to repeatedly hijack your time. But it's important to set aside your agenda when necessary. If you, like me, prefer to have a plan and work the plan, can you sometimes let go of your attachment to the plan?

Sometimes the most productive thing you can do is to be present with someone. If you want to be practical about it, a meaningful pastoral conversation can pay dividends for years. In addition, sometimes it's simply the right thing to do. You can't plan when a door will open unexpectedly in a relationship. But you can be present to walk through it if it does.

Not every pastor has a spouse or children at home. If you do, a single-minded focus on work can take a toll on your family. When I was in college, I spent a summer on a mission project. The team leader often promised his children he would spend time with them later. He never followed through. Not surprisingly, they acted out to get his attention. That was one lesson.

By contrast, my mother told stories of growing up with my grandfather, a pastor. Gramps always had his office in the home. His door was always open to his five children. She never forgot it. That was another lesson.

If you have a family, how can you be more present to them? Here are five ideas:

1. Turn your phone completely off at times when you are home, especially during meals.

2. If you have children, take them out individually.

3. Have dinner together at least twice a week.

4. Don't talk about church at dinner.

5. Don't multitask when family members are talking to you. (Research shows you can't read and listen.)

3. **When doing interferes with natural processes.** Some things simply take time. You can have a vision, goals, and an action plan, and something still doesn't work out. Then you let it go and you see a breakthrough. This can happen with worship, staff development, your relationships with key individuals, and the financial life of the church. You can't predict what will happen. You can't try harder to make it happen. You simply have to wait.

This happens often in organizational life. In several of my consultations with congregations, it seemed they hadn't gotten far in a process. Then a year later, I checked in, and amazing things were happening. They had developed a plan with my help. They may or may not have followed the plan. Still, the results were aligned with what we had worked on together, just as they hoped.

It also happens in relationships. You can work like crazy to heal a relationship with someone who is a challenge. Or you and someone else simply aren't in sync. You have meeting after meeting, yet nothing changes. Then you decide there's nothing more you can do. A month or a year later, something has shifted.

I can't explain all of this. However, I do know that everything has many causes. One action can affect many other pieces. Many factors are at work, even in myself, that I know nothing about.

Letting go of an outcome may be the most productive thing you can do. But how do you know when to push through and when to wait? If you have consistently been taking action, say for three to six months, on something that is not going anywhere, stop. Consider taking a break, whether it's a ministry initiative or a relationship you'd like to improve. You may want to spend your energy elsewhere for a time.

4. **When productivity becomes an end in itself.** Remember, productivity is not the most important thing. Productivity is *for* something: making progress in ministry and reaching your goals. You want to get things done for a purpose.

Perhaps one symptom of this problem is the constant quest for new systems. I'm prone to this myself. I recently downloaded an app a friend recommended. Then made myself delete it. I didn't need another thing to learn. You, too, may find yourself trying this app and that program. It takes time to implement a new system. That takes time away from actually taking action toward your goals. Any system will work if you work it. Pick one and use it for at least six months.

Keep lifting your head up a little higher and keep the end in mind. Make sure your systems serve you. If you are a paper person, don't be ashamed. (I love paper.) If it works for you, great. Don't waste energy thinking you should be doing it electronically. If you love electronics, terrific. Find an app and stick with it.

The Secret of Sabbath: Why Rest Is Good for Your Ministry

When was the last time you took a real Sabbath? Or even a real day off when you did no church work at all? It's hard to sustain ministry over time without rest.

Think about it. We are:

- Leaders in church, community, and denomination

- Administrators

- Preachers

- Teachers

- Counselors

- Liturgists/officiants

- Writers

- Representatives of God to our people and to our wider community

Those are a lot of roles to fill without enough rest.

Here are three reasons why you need a Sabbath:

1. It's biblical.

2. It's biological.

3. It's better for everybody.

1. **It's biblical.** I know you know this. In the creation story in Genesis, God rests. *God rests.* We're so used to the story we may not even notice

it. If God takes time off in the story, what's the message for us? Work constantly? No.

It's in the New Testament too. One of my favorite passages is in Mk 6:31-32, where Jesus says, "Come away to a deserted place all by yourselves and rest a while." The text goes on, "For many were coming and going, and they had no leisure even to eat. And they went away in the boat to a deserted place by themselves."

I know, I know. The people follow them, and Jesus ends up feeding the 5,000. But still. Jesus called them aside when they were too busy to eat. (When was the last time you ate in your car?) He could have said, "We just don't have time." Jesus also goes off by himself for prayer and quiet.

When I was in my twenties, I heard someone do a monologue about Jesus and his disciples playing in the water. At first, it was a shock to think about Jesus splashing and laughing with his disciples. Yet it stuck with me. It rang true.

When was the last time you played at anything?[3]

2. **It's biological.** First, our bodies need rest. We need sleep, and we live in a culture where sleep is not valued. I've never had a high tolerance for sleep deprivation. I have to go to bed at a decent hour because otherwise I simply don't do well. When I read about sleep research, I realize I'm blessed. Even for those who can tolerate sleep deprivation, it takes a toll over time.

Athletes know this: They train, and then they rest. So do musicians. Musician and psychologist Noa Kageyama suggests "4 Signs You May Be Practicing Too Hard." These might apply to clergy who aren't getting enough rest, too.

- **Negative Mood.** You feel persistently cranky.

- **Perceived Effort.** Everything feels harder.

- **Recovery.** You don't recover, even when you take a day off.

- **Performance Quality.** You can't do your job as well as you normally do.[4]

Second, our brains need rest. Research on productivity and creativity shows that when we turn our attention to something else, we may find solutions for problems. Our brain needs "downtime."[5]

When I was preaching every week, I took Fridays off. I would finish my sermon on Thursdays and come home and say, "This is terrible!" I would let it go, take the Friday off. Somehow when I looked at the sermon again on Saturday, I could immediately see how to fix the problem. Sometimes I could even see there wasn't really a problem. It was fine.

Kenneth Atchity in *Write Time* suggests using unconscious processes in our work. When we let work sit, something happens even though we do not consciously think about it. Atchity says, "The benefits of vacations are immeasurable. The longer an idea 'percolates' in the mind the greater its chances of being expressed clearly and powerfully when the time is right." I'm grateful I read this book before I started preaching every week. What Atchity describes was my experience as a preacher. I still experience it as a writer.[6]

Brett and Kate McKay recommend a "Tech Sabbath." Their blog "The Art of Manliness" may be targeting men, but this is good advice for everyone. True confession: I haven't done this fully. But I almost never check work email on Sunday. (Then again, I'm not working in a church right now. Pick your own best day.) Next step for me: taking *two* days off from email.[7]

If you feel overwhelmed by your workload, I recommend you immediately start taking more time off. It doesn't have to be a lot more time. I do suggest at least one full day without doing anything (much) for church. As someone in one of my coaching groups said, "There are no program emergencies." It's one thing to respond to a death or other pastoral care crisis. Most other issues can wait a day.

Sometimes being overwhelmed simply comes from fatigue. It's harder to think clearly. It takes longer to write the sermon. The challenges are more upsetting. Creativity goes down. Getting rest is worth it simply from a practical point of view. You'll get things done faster.

3. **It's better for everybody.** The most mature, well-functioning people know they are not indispensable. Sabbath is about boundaries. Boundaries between work and not-work. Between us and our people. Between our family time and church.

Boundaries don't have to be rigid. Overly rigid boundaries are the flip side of having none. They are an anxious response. You may decide to respond to something on your day off, but don't automatically assume you should or must. Conversely, you don't want to say, "NEVER call me on my day off."

Sabbath is good for you for several reasons:

- It gives you rest—perhaps even time for a nap.

- It gives you space.

- Letting things go is a spiritual practice. If you think everything depends on you and you can't take even one day away, you are overfunctioning.

- You will have to focus more during the time you *are* working to get the Sabbath time.

When you take Sabbath time, it's better for others too:

- They have to figure things out without you.

- They will get your best when you are present.

- They will have to be thoughtful: Should I contact the pastor or not?

- Your family knows they can count on your attention on that day.

Make choices about your use of electronic communication on your days off. The expectation of immediate response is growing, and that's not a good thing. Think through your principles about email, texting, and returning calls, especially during your time off. One pastor I coach doesn't check church email on his day off. He has a different address for personal matters.

Reality check: I know you may have life circumstances apart from church demands that make this difficult. If you are bivocational or have small children, a chronically ill spouse, or elderly parents, that can take up most of your extra time. Plus, the laundry has to get done sometime.

For people who have heavy personal responsibilities in addition to church, I don't want to make Sabbath one more obligation. I do hope you sustain yourself in the middle of the challenges. Can you cover your responsibilities and allow an hour or two each week to do something that gives you joy and renews your spirit? Can you ask for help, at church or at home?

I also know there are seasons in church life when it is harder to take time off. At the same time, I've met pastors who've lived for years without adequate respite. I don't recommend it. You will be exhausted. And when you retire, you won't know what to do with yourself. You will not have much of a "self" apart from your work. You won't have many relationships outside your ministry.

What I want is for you to keep going over time with strength and with joy. Enough rest, refreshment, and enjoyment will help you do that. It benefits everyone.

Questions for Reflection

What do you want to focus your attention on in your ministry now? What are your short-term intentions (90 days or so)?

How do you think you can increase your focus during working hours?

What can you stop doing now?

What time do you take off every day? Every week? Every year?

What gives you joy in ministry? Are you doing it, at least some of the time?

8

Get Prayerful
What Matters in Ministry?

Catholic cardinal Timothy Dalton told a story about Pope John XXIII:

Every night about midnight he'd kneel at the altar and say: "Lord, here are the things I am ready to take a bottle of grappa over." And he'd list all the crises of the day. Then, he'd say: "Lord, it's Your Church, not mine. I did the best I could. I'm going to bed now." And he was done for the day.[1]

A well-grounded spiritual life will help sustain you, no matter what is going on. Prayer is a resource to help you discern and persist. Prayer can help you let go of the outcome. Rather than "I ought to pray more," you might think, "Prayer will help me with my ministry more than anything else I can do."

Prayerfully Discern

Discernment is a critical element in ministry. You have to answer questions that will determine how you move forward in the long term and day to day.

You face big questions such as:

- What is my purpose—in the short term and long term?

- How is God leading me as we move forward?

- How is God leading us as a community?

- Should I stay or go?

- Will our congregation survive into the future? Will the wider church survive?

And daily questions such as:

- What should I do today? What should I do right now?

- How do I best support this parishioner in crisis?

- Is this criticism a learning opportunity for me or mindless pushback—or both?

- Should I say yes or no to this request?

You won't always know if you have the "right" answer to any one of these questions. However, you have to make decisions and take action. Prayer is a vital element in discernment, in your life and in the life of your community. Moreover, if you have an ongoing prayer life, you will find it easier to turn to prayer when inevitable setbacks happen.

Prayer can help you determine the principles on which you make your decisions. Prayer can support you as you move forward in living out the decisions.[2]

Listening in Prayer

Discernment requires you to listen to your deepest self. You do need to listen to others, as we've discussed. Even more important is listening to God. In the middle of the busy life of ministry, it's tough to make time for prayer at all, let alone get quiet enough to *listen* in prayer.

Consider incorporating some meditative prayer into your life. Even two minutes of listening to God can help you stay centered. Listening to God is always of value. Here are a couple of key benefits for our purposes:

- It can help you stay grounded as you answer the questions above and the others that arise every day.

- Listening to God can also help you discern who needs your listening ear. As you sit quietly in prayer, notice who comes to mind. Pay attention to the internal nudge you feel.

Most pastors love to talk. We talk to God in prayer, whether publicly or privately. Listening to God is also important. I recommend you at least try meditative or contemplative prayer. Here's the truth. I find it challenging. Still, I do a little of it almost every day. My mind is a busy one, and I think that's true of all of us. I've meditated daily for 20 minutes for years, and not at all for years. I'm at the five-minute range at the moment.

Quiet prayer is challenging. Yet over time, it can calm you. It benefits you not only when you are praying but throughout the rest of your day. It helps you settle down emotionally and spiritually to discern what to do. You don't have to be really good at it to benefit from it. In a way, no one is "good" at it. That's why it's a practice.

If meditative prayer isn't for you, it's okay. You're not failing at prayer. One of my most prayerful friends and colleagues says she just can't do it. I share other options for prayer later in this chapter.

There's an additional benefit to the practice of meditation. Listening to God will help you listen better to others. When you are quiet before God, you can learn to be present with others in a different way.

Getting Help with Prayerful Discernment

You don't have to go it alone. An outside perspective can also be useful. I mentioned in Chapter 4 people who can support you such as coaches and therapists. A spiritual director can be another important resource. I've had more than one through my ministry. I worked with my most recent spiritual director monthly for well over a decade. We talked about all aspects of my life, including family and work. In addition, he always asked me about my prayer and worship life. It reminded me to keep that aspect of my life a priority. He helped me think through the decisions in front of me, large and small. He would remind me that I was doing better than I thought at everything, including prayer.

As a Baptist, I didn't know about spiritual direction early in my ministry. It's more widely known now in Protestant circles. I've since met a number of Baptists who are themselves spiritual directors. My own most recent spiritual director was Roman Catholic, a former priest. However, he said almost all the people he worked with were Protestants.

Connect with people from other traditions to learn about different ways to pray. I had one coaching client, an Episcopal priest in a highly liturgical church. He offered to light candles when he knew there was a need. The church had Mass and prayers for individuals every single day. When two family members had health crises in one year, I asked him to light candles. My parents might have been shocked, but this new practice was comforting.

And remember, you are not the only "pray-er" in your ministry setting. It's not all up to you. You can rely on spiritually mature members for prayer support, even if there's only one. Earlier I mentioned Ethel, a key leader who would invite me for coffee at McDonald's. I always knew Ethel was praying for me and for the church. It's not that I thought then or now that prayer was a magic bullet. But I knew even then that prayerful people in key positions could make a difference.

Discernment isn't once for all. It's ongoing. The big decisions have to be made and acted on. As you live them out, you make more decisions about how to move forward. Here's the sequence: Pray. Decide. Take action. Reflect on what you learned. Repeat.

Prayerfully Persist

Wherever you are in your ministry, the practice of prayer can help you. You may be at the beginning or end. You may be excited or discouraged. You may feel energized or exhausted. You need energy, character, creativity, and plain stubbornness to persist. Even a minute here or there of prayer can help.

Here are some approaches to prayer that are worth trying. Any of them can help you put one foot in front of the other as you move forward with God's work.

1. Pray your calendar.

Do this monthly, weekly, and daily as you plan.

Approach your schedule with prayer rather than the frantic sense you will never do it all. It will help you thoughtfully choose your priorities. You know you can't do it all. That means making choices. Don't go it alone. Ask God for help on what to do and—even more importantly—what not to do.

Consider stopping in the middle of the day to recalibrate. If your schedule changes, stop and think: What do I want to do for the rest of the day? What inner direction do I sense? Kirk Byron Jones suggests you stop for prayer every day at noon.[3] Noonday prayer is a long-established practice in some traditions.

It's not simply about being more productive. The message may be this: Do less. Go home. Rest. Take a nap. Or it might be to spend a block of time with this needy person and let the to-do list go.

2. Practice intercessory prayer.

You'll find it easier to persist in ministry if you pray for your people and for the ministry. You can pray for leaders and potential leaders, for your staff, and for those in difficulties. This doesn't take hours. A few minutes daily or a few more minutes weekly will help you keep going. Angela Ashwin has a wonderful template for daily prayer:

I give thanks . . .

I confess . . .

I ask for help and guidance . . .

I pray for those I love . . . for people I encounter in my daily life
. . . for those carrying responsibilities . . . for those in need or
distress . . .[4]

I've heard it said that ministry would be great if it weren't for the people. Not everyone, of course, but those few people who take up our time and energy. They even live in our thoughts even when we're not with them. Try this: Pray for them more. You never know how God can work in their hearts. And you can be sure that God will work in yours if you are able to pray for them. All you have to do is mention their name in prayer.

Family therapist Peggy Treadwell once said that you can never be cut off from people if you are praying for them.[5] If people aren't talking to you or have left the church, you can still pray for them. You can at least mention them to God in prayer, if nothing more. This applies to difficult family members, too.

3. Take a silent retreat.

I once went on a 24-hour silent pastors' retreat with my Baptist colleagues. We had a wonderful time. However, we chatty Baptists couldn't quite make it through that last silent meal. We ended up with 23 hours of silence. It was well worth it.

Roman Catholics have a long tradition of silent retreats. Their retreat centers are a wonderful resource. Most Protestant "retreats" involve lots of chatter, and they have their own value. However, give a silent retreat a try at least once. Our routines have little opportunity for extended times of prayer. For most pastors, the only way to get that time is to get out of town. It can be a wonderful antidote for chatty but exhausted clergy.[6]

4. Pray while walking or running

For some pastors, sitting still is like pulling teeth. I've known a number of clergy who run or walk daily and use that as their prayer time. I met one pastor from the upper Midwest who even ran in winter on ice with special shoes. She prayed throughout. The rhythm of your gait acts like a prayer word or phrase to help you keep your mind on your prayer.

Even if you love sitting down to pray like I do, give movement a try. I do walk almost every day. While that's not my main prayer time, bringing my mind back to God as I walk is a blessing.

Another option is SLOW prayer walking. Instead of using your usual exercise time, you take a very slow walk. You pay close attention to your movements. The feeling of your foot on the floor. The swing of your arms. As you do this, you can give thanks to God for the ability to move.

If you are not able to walk much for physical reasons, you can bring your awareness to every movement. If you can't walk, you can cultivate awareness of every movement you are able to make. Anyone can use movement as a means of prayer.

5. Pray with others

For extroverts who dislike alone time, group prayer can be a wonderful practice. For introverts, it can be a structured way to be with others, easier than coffee hour.

I know people who have participated in prayer groups for years. They occur in person and on Zoom now. For example, the Shalem Center offers regular virtual prayer times and other offerings. Contemplative Outreach is an international organization with a global network of virtual and in-person gatherings for the practice of centering prayer.[7]

Here are a number of options for group prayer:

- Centering/meditative prayer

- Intercessory prayer with colleagues, staff, or church members

- Praying with your partner

- Praying with your board

Prayerfully Let Go

The Dalai Lama shared a letter with his followers on March 30, 2020. He said, "I take great solace in the following wise advice to examine the problems before us: 'If there is something to be done—do it, without any need to worry; if there's nothing to be done, worrying about it further will not help.'"[8] It's good advice for Christian leaders, too. I've written this on a card. I put it in a place where I come across it regularly. I reflect on these words, in my own life and as I think about the wider church and the world. It's a good reminder to focus on myself and what I can do in the moment.

Pastoral leaders feel a lot of pressure right now. We know the church we love is struggling, at the congregational level and more broadly. The people in congregations are anxious. They project onto their leadership the responsibility for making it all work. However, it does not help to worry about matters we don't control, as the Dalai Lama points out.

What does help? Look for what you *can* do. Get clear about what you are called to do right now, in the short term. Find the places you have agency and take small actions. Keep it simple. One pastor, Rev. Rick Mixon, said this about his own calling: "For such a time as this, I may be called simply to care for the people in my charge. I don't have to be Moses or Elijah or the second coming of Jesus to be a faithful shepherd for my flock."[9]

Leaders need to let go of the outcome. It's difficult when we care so much about the ministry and want to make it work. We can imagine that vision, and the potential impact on our community. However, letting go can be the best way to make room for something new to happen. "The wind blows where it chooses, and you hear the sound of it, but you do not know where it comes from or where it goes. So it is with everyone who is born of the Spirit." (Jn 3:8). The work of the Holy Spirit is unexpected, unpredictable. If you cling to a specific outcome, you may get in the way of God's work in the world.

Orthodox theologian John Chryssavgis put it this way: ". . . prayer is the realization that what matters most is not success. Prayer is the acceptance of frailty and failure—first within ourselves, and then in the world around us. . . . Prayer is learning to live, without expecting to see results; it is learning to love, without hoping to see return; it is learning to be, without demanding to have."[10]

Here are some ways to let go:

Accept. Multiple forces are at work in your church, in the community, and in the wider world. I know from experience how easy it is to think, *If I were just a better leader, everything would go better/ the church would have more people/more money/more ministries.* You do the best you can. You recognize how many things are out of your control. You face not only the big trends in church life right now. You also have decades or more of history in your specific congregation. You have your contribution to make, and you have your limitations.

If you cling to the outcome, you will be constantly exhausted and frustrated. I don't believe making things happen is your call as a leader. I absolutely believe in clear vision, goals, and action plans. However, you can't predict the results of those plans when they are carried out. The unexpected happens: you meet someone. Or someone gets a new idea. Or new resources become available. Things take half as long—or more likely, twice as long. Or we discover that a certain goal needs to be adapted. The landscape has changed suddenly or gradually.

Martha Tatarnic, rector of St. George's Anglican Church in St. Catharines [*sic*], Ontario, learned about what's called "ultrarealism" from long-distance running. She says,

"Ultrarealism . . . sees, accepts, and embraces what actually is. I might get freaked out about my uneven breathing. I might feel despair about the spitting rain and how slowly the first mile seems to have gone when I still have seventeen to go. But while these things . . . might be true, I can choose to note that, right here in this present moment, my leg muscles feel strong, the rain is refreshing, and I have the great privilege of being able to run."

Tatarnic applies this to her own work: "My job description is amazingly simple: my job is to lift up." She literally lifts up the bread and wine. And she lifts up real stories which also communicate God's presence. "That's the job."[11]

Claim your work. Your call is to show up and do the work God has called you to. Your call is to occupy your role as a leader with grace and creativity. Live out that call, in the place where you are, just for today.

It is a deeply spiritual practice to open our hearts to those we serve, without judgment. It's a practice to serve without a sense that it is all up to us. It's a practice to let go of saving the world, or even our church. You can do the work that God has uniquely gifted you to do without a Messiah complex. In fact, you can do the work better. Without the intense pressure to make things come out your way, you will have more freedom to be creative. You will have more room to be yourself, your true self.

Margaret Wheatley talks about the challenges of working for good in today's world. She suggests that courage is vital, and she talks about what she calls "*warriors*." She means those who have the courage to keep going, even if they don't know what the result will be.

Despite the difficulties, Wheatley says, "We do not give up our work. We act with greater clarity and courage once freed from oppressive ambition. And we cheerfully choose a new role, transforming from savior to warrior."[12] I would add that for Christian leaders, we don't need to **be** the savior because we **have** one.

I was raised with a deep sense of responsibility. You probably were too. The idea of letting go in this way seems irresponsible at first glance. I've learned over the years my call is to be responsible *for myself*. When I do that, I'm more present with others and more engaged with my true work.

What are you called to do? Can you wake up every day and do it?

Take the long view. Everything of value takes time. You never know the long-term results of your work, in your congregation and individual lives. Peggy Treadwell once told the story of the Episcopal priest at her childhood church in Georgia. He came to the train station with her family to see her off to college. She was heading north to go to school, unusual at that time. More than 30 years later, she remembered her priest's presence at a pivotal moment. She told a group of clergy never to underestimate the impact of their work. I heard the story 20 years ago, and I still remember that priest at the train station.[13]

Pray in a Way That Works for You

My friend and colleague Rev. Cindy Maybeck prays during the night. She's always dealt with insomnia. She says, "It gets rid of the pressure of how I'm going to find time to pray. For years, I fussed about the insomnia." Now she sees it this way: "God wakes me up to talk to me." She adds, "There's never anything else scheduled at four in the morning." Then she goes back to sleep. Cindy's pattern of prayer wouldn't work for me. I've always prayed first thing in the morning. I can't do it at night, and I can't do it in the middle of the night. I'm a morning person. Even in college I got up for breakfast. Morning has been my prayer time for 40 years.

Start small. If you don't have a practice of prayer right now, start small—as in *really* small.

Here are five ideas:

1.   Try one minute of meditation.

2.   Pray for one member of your board every day.

3. Prayerfully read one verse of Scripture.

4. Pray while you walk from your car into the church. If you walk or bike to church, use a little of that time to pray.

5. Take ten prayerful breaths when you wake up, in the middle of the day or the middle of the night. (You could breathe in on "The Lord is my shepherd" and out on "I shall not want.")

Questions for Reflection

What might God be asking me to do **today** (including what I can do for myself)?

What is my prayer practice now? What practice might I try out?

What other spiritual practices do I or might I include? (Possibilities to consider: Worship you don't lead, Bible study beyond preaching prep, lectio divina/praying with Scripture, fasting.)

What is God calling me to accept:

At church?

In my family?

In the world at large?

What is my work right now?

Where can I look back now and see God's hand at work. (Even though I didn't see it at the time.)

We Are All, Always, Enough

Soprano Barbara Cook played the original Marian the Librarian on Broadway in the musical *The Music Man*. She once held a master class here in Portland. She told the students about an early experience she had:

". . . I was standing in the wings, waiting to go on and audition, and I was and am a very nervous kind of person . . . everybody who sang before me had a better voice, looked prettier, had a better figure . . . it occurred to me that day that if I could find a way to really learn who I am and put that into my work, then there could be no real competition, because I could only compete with myself, because there's only one of me."

Cook used to tell her students, "It's hard to believe, whatever you're doing, that you're enough. We are *all*, always enough."[14]

It is hard to believe you are enough in these days of discerning how to do church in a new world. How to adapt the traditions of the past to meet the needs of the present. How to develop new ministries for a new day. How to fund ministry now and into the future. How to meet the countless needs within the congregation and in your community. It never feels like enough.

On the days you think for a moment it's enough, someone from your church tells you it's not. And the next day you compare yourself with your colleagues who are doing such creative outreach. Or they seem calm through the ups and downs while you're going nuts.

Many of the pastors I talk to are far harder on themselves than on other people. They say things to themselves they would never say to others. I hope you extend the same grace to yourself that you offer to others.

I hope you can learn more deeply who you are. Then put that into your work more and more. Sure, you have plenty to learn and lots of ways to grow. You can fill in all the caveats for yourself.

May you believe that who you are and what you offer are enough to fulfill God's call on your life, for now.

Note to the Reader

Thank you for reading *Sustainable Ministry*. May God carry you as you do your work. My prayers are with you.

Don't stop here! On the following pages, you will find additional tools to help you persist in ministry. You will also find recommended resources, including books and digital offerings. I also include recommended clergy training programs. It takes more than a book to sustain yourself for the long term. These programs can help you put these ideas to work in your own ministry.

You can find me at margaretmarcuson.com.

And don't forget to take a nap.

Appendix A

Sustain Yourself in Ministry: An Inventory

(Find a downloadable version at margaretmarcuson.com/sustainablem inistry)

How are you doing at keeping yourself going in ministry? Take this quick assessment to check it out.

Give yourself a number from 1 to 10 on the following. A meaningful ministry does not require 10's! ("A" students take note.)

____ I know what I want in my ministry and my life. I know my top values.

____ I know my most important priorities (personal and professional) for the next quarter. I don't have too many.

____ I keep the long view in mind. I know progress in ministry is measured in years not days. I am not overly attached to a particular outcome or time frame.

____ I can calmly articulate my own priorities for the church's ministry to leaders and to the congregation.

____ I am well connected with key leaders, other significant members and with staff.

____ I manage relationships with people who disagree with me or appear difficult. I can stay in touch even when it is challenging.

____ I don't take (too much) responsibility for others. I know that everyone is responsible for themselves.

____ I take responsibility for my own role, commitments, and relationships.

____ I expect resistance when I move forward as a leader. I'm not shocked when it happens.

____ I work to depersonalize criticism. I recognize that some of it goes with my role and is inevitable.

____ I know what I need to do to calm myself when my emotional buttons get pushed at church.

____ I understand my role and responsibilities in relation to stewardship and finances. I am in touch with the financial facts of my congregation. I have solid relationships with the financial leaders.

____ I have spiritual practices and habits which sustain me.

____ I take time off each week. I take all my vacation. I have interests outside the church. I have some time when I am not available.

____ I use all my continuing education time and budget.

____ I am part of a group of thoughtful colleagues. They can provide me with objective feedback when I am faced with a ministry or personal challenge.

____ I have a coach, mentor and/or colleague who can help me reflect on challenges that arise.

____ I recognize I share the responsibility for the work of ministry with the congregation and its leaders. I don't feel the weight of the future of this church (or the wider church). I know it's not all up to me.

Ask yourself:

- What's solidly in place? Celebrate what is right!

- What support elements do you still need?

- And what's your biggest challenge right now? How might you take one small step forward?

Appendix B
"What Do You Want" Planning Guide

(A downloaded version of this guide and an expanded version can be found at margaretmarcuson.com/sustainableministry.)

Leadership starts with you. One of the best ways to work on it is to ask yourself, "*What do I want?*" However, you may ask, "Isn't ministry about what **God** wants, not me? Isn't it a little selfish to ask myself what **I** want?" You don't ask that question in isolation. You prayerfully discern. And you consult and collaborate as you move forward.

Remember: "Take delight in the Lord, and he will give you the desires of your heart." Psalm 37:4 (NRSV)

Here's a process to help you start to discern what you want and make a plan to move forward. You can do it in one day. If you can get out of the office, so much the better. Or you can do one step every day for a week. If you plan better with others, you could take a retreat day with colleagues. Or you could do a daily call to work on each step.

Suggested Process

Step 1 (or Day 1)

Read Scripture and pray for guidance. (Try Psalm 23, Phil. 4:6-7, or another passage that is meaningful to you.)

If you are comfortable practicing contemplative prayer, try this:

In-breath: Lead me, O Lord, in your righteousness

Out-breath: make your way straight before me.

Even if this is a new practice for you, try it for a minute. Or 5 minutes. Write for 5–10 minutes on this statement: "I am called to . . ." Or another option is to ask: "What is the best use of my life, given this much blessing?" Then look out the window or go outside, weather permitting.

Then quickly draft a short purpose statement for your ministry right now or your life as a whole. You don't have to get it right. It doesn't have to take hours. You could even set your phone timer for 2–5 minutes. Then take a break (or leave it overnight.)

Step 2 (or Day 2)

Take another look at your purpose statement. Revise to make it more fully reflect who you are and what your call is.

Take the list of ministry visioning questions. Answer them one by one. You can come up with more than one answer for each question. For some, it will be easy to generate many answers. Let yourself freely generate ideas. Include the everyday and the impossible.

Ministry visioning questions (Adapted from Dave Ellis) See his book, *Falling Awake: Creating the Life of Your Dreams* for a comprehensive life planning process (Breakthrough Enterprises, 2002, or get a free pdf at https://fallingawake.com/all-books/).

What do you want?

What do you want for your ministry? (This can get harder as you go further out in time. However, if you stick with it, it can lead to answers that can improve your life and ministry significantly. It will help you develop a long-term perspective.)

- What do you want this week?

- What do you want this month?

- What do you want this year?

- What do you want during the next 5 years?

- What do you want for the next 10 years?

- What do you want for the next 25 years (for this church, even if you leave sooner? And for yourself)?

- What do you want for the next 50 years (for the church and the world at large)?

Step 3 (or Day 3, or more)

What do you want in every category of your ministry?

Answer the questions that give you energy to consider. If your heart sinks at the prospect of considering one category, skip it. You can come back later *if you want.*

This step will take a little longer. If you're doing the process day to day, you might spread it over a few days.

You might consider these questions:

What do you want the ministry to have? (circumstances, results)

What do you want the people to do? (actions, activities)

Who do you want them to be? (values, attitudes)

- Worship

- Outreach

- The spiritual growth of your people

- Pastoral care

- Money (your salary, giving, spending, managing, giving beyond the congregation)

- The building

- Leadership development

- Educational ministry

- Relationships

- Generational ministries (children, youth, young adults, older adults)

- Music

- Staff

- Anything else that is important to you in ministry

Step 4 (or Day 4)

Set aside your notes, and spend some time in prayer. You can repeat the centering prayer above. Or use the words of a gospel song, like this:

In-breath: Guide my feet

Out-breath: while I run this race.

Or pray in whatever way works for you. Pray in words. Meditate. Use a prayer from a prayer book.

Read the purpose statement again. Place your hand on your heart and ask God, "Is this my purpose?" See what further insight you gain, and adapt. Remember, it doesn't have to be perfect. An imperfect purpose can help you move forward.

Reflect on the times in your ministry when you've had the greatest joy. Notice the thoughts and feelings that come into your mind.

Go back to your answers to the ministry visioning questions. Take a few moments with each answer. Notice which ones give you energy. Do you feel the sense of joy you remember from other times in your ministry? Mark those. Let go for now of thoughts of how to do it. Let go of thinking, "I could never do that/get that/have that." And set aside the ones that smack of obligation or "should-ness." Ministry has plenty of obligations without you adding more.

Step 5 (or Day 5)

Now, prayerfully review the ones that give you energy. Keep your purpose in mind. Ask yourself, "What do I want to do now?" Make one list. "What do I want to do in one year?" Make another list. "What do I want to do in three to five years?" And finally, "What do I want to do before I die?"

Now look at the items you want to do now. Choose the items you are truly committed to moving forward on. Maybe you want to make a big leap in your preaching. Or take your day off every week. Or start to sing again. Or spend more time in the community. Or work with key leaders to learn about community needs to start a new outreach.

Step 6 (or Day 6)

Start making plans.

Try this: Take the idea to do right away that excites you the most:

Let's take one idea, say, improve your preaching, as an example. Remember, choose this only if this idea gives you joy!

Ask yourself:

How do I improve my preaching?

Write down as many ideas as you can. Don't be afraid to make some of them out of the ordinary or a little crazy. And write down the ordinary ones, too. Twenty is not too many! Three is not enough.

For example:

- Spend half an hour more in preparation.

- Hire a coach.

- Join Toastmasters.

- Ask someone in the congregation I trust for feedback.

- Partner with a colleague.

- Read a preaching book.

- Try a different method each Sunday for a month: manuscript, outline, Mind Map, note cards, no notes.

- Watch preachers I admire on YouTube.

- Preach from the back of the church.

- Sing a sermon.

If you have a crazy idea, try to make a good one out of it. Singing a sermon, for example, could be a good idea. Or at least sing it when you practice it.

Of the ones you like, you can make them more specific.

For example:

How do I partner with a colleague?

- Pick someone I like.

- Pick someone who's a challenge.

- Pick someone from my denomination.

- Pick someone from another denomination.

- Video sermons and exchange.

- Do a pulpit exchange and get feedback from the other preacher's members.

- Read a preaching book together and implement the ideas.

You get the idea.

Step 7 (or Day 7)

Review your ideas. Choose the ones that sound the most fun or helpful. Look for what you *want* to do, not what you think you *ought* to do. Schedule them:

Email Fred on Tuesday about a pulpit exchange.

A plan can be made surprisingly quickly. It doesn't have to be perfect, only enough to get you going. Even a few new items can help you have more energy for your ministry. Some you are already doing. You can try them in a different way.

Prayerfully offer this purpose and these hopes, dreams, and plans to God. Before you end, decide what you are going to do tomorrow to move forward.

Appendix C
Staff Planning Questionnaire

(A downloadable version can be found at margaretmarcuson.com/sust ainableministry)

Most churches have staff in addition to the pastor. Managing a church staff can be a challenge. Most of us had no training in how to supervise. We have to learn on the job.

Here are some questions to help you think through your work with your staff:

- How clear am I about my ministry direction this year and for the long term?

- What portions of this do I still need to communicate with staff? When will I do so?

- How clear are roles and responsibilities for our staff?

- What do we still need to do to make them clearer?

- Who needs to be involved?

- When will I start on this?

- What are ways I can invite more constructive feedback from staff? How might I enjoy that process?

- What are my ideas for staying in touch with staff members this month? This year?

- What would be fun?

- What do I intend to do about staff meetings?

- Where is my own anxiety focused right now?

- Where do I see signs of reactivity in the staff?

- What's going on in the larger church system that might be triggering it?

- What can I do to keep a little calmer in staff relations right now?

- What are my own strengths for leading my staff?

Appendix D
Money/Stewardship Tips

1. **Clarify** your own principles about giving. You will find it easier to invite others to give.

2. **Define** your own views in your stewardship sermons. View them as opportunities for the congregation to hear what you think.

3. **Acknowledge** your own challenges in this area. Stand side-by-side with them in receiving God's invitation to give.

4. **Share** the responsibility for stewardship with others. Don't be the only one lying awake at night. If there are challenges, they are not yours alone.

5. **Keep** your sense of humor around the stewardship process. If you feel anxious or frustrated, do your best to lighten up about it.

6. **Look** for others who also have a sense of humor. Then recruit them to serve in the area of stewardship. They will help you keep a sense of perspective.

7. **Be honest** with the congregation about financial challenges. Don't whine and bemoan the situation. But don't protect them from the realities of congregational life.

8. **Track** pledging and giving patterns over the years. Facts, even if they are difficult facts, can help lower anxiety.

9. **Connect** your own vision for ministry with the stewardship process. Do it both in your own mind and in what you say to others. Over time, this can help raise the level of the conversation.

10. **Maintain** a focus on stewardship through the year. Don't limit it to a few weeks in fall or spring. This can broaden the focus beyond support for the annual budget.

RECOMMENDED RESOURCES

Books

Pastoral Ministry

Creech, Robert. *Family Systems and Congregational Life: A Map for Ministry*. Grand Rapids: Baker Academic, 2019.

Ferguson, Todd W. and Josh Packard. *Stuck: Why Clergy Are Alienated from Their Calling, Congregation, and Career…and What to Do about It*. Minneapolis: Fortress, 2022.

Friedman, Edwin. *A Failure of Nerve: Leadership in the Age of the Quick Fix*, ed. Margaret M. Treadwell and Edward W. Beal. New York: Seabury, 2007.

Friedman, Edwin. *Generation to Generation*. New York: Guilford, 1985.

Galindo, Israel, ed. *Leadership in Ministry: Bowen Theory in the Congregational Context*. Didache, 2017.

Galindo, Israel, ed. *Reframing Ministry Leadership: New Insights from a Systems Theory Perspective*. Didache, 2023.

Galindo, Israel, ed. *When a Pastor Is Fired: Addressing the Silent Epidemic of Forced Terminations in Ministry*. Didache, 2025.

Marcuson, Margaret. *Leaders Who Last*. New York: Seabury, 2009.

Rendle, Gil and Susan Beaumont. *When Moses Met Aaron: Staffing and Supervision in the Larger Church*. Herndon, VA: Alban, 2007. (Note: not just for large churches).

Richardson, Ronald W. *Polarization and the Healthier Church*. 2012.

Finances and Stewardship

Copeland, Adam J., ed. *Beyond the Offering Plate: A Holistic Approach to Stewardship*. Louisville: Westminster John Knox, 2017.

Jamieson, Janet T. and Philip D. *Ministry and Money: A Practical Guide for Pastors*. Louisville: Westminster John Knox, 2009.

Lane, Charles R. and Grace Duddy Pomroy. *Embracing Stewardship*. 2016.

Marcuson, Margaret. *Money and Your Ministry*. Portland: Marcuson Leadership Circle, 2014.

Personal Growth and Bowen Family Systems Theory

Brown, Jenny. *Growing Yourself Up: How to Bring Your Best to All of Life's Relationships*. Chatswood, NSW: Exisle, 2nd edition, 2017.

Ellis, Dave. *Falling Awake: Creating the Life of Your Dreams*. Rapid City, SD: Breakthrough Enterprises, 2002.

Galindo, Israel, Elaine Boomer, and Don Reagan. *A Family Genogram Workbook*. Educational Consultants, 2006.

Gilbert, Roberta. *The Eight Concepts of Bowen Theory*. Falls Church and Basye, Virginia: Leading Systems Press, 2006.

Gilbert, Roberta. *Extraordinary Relationships*. Minneapolis: Chronimed, 1992.

Harrison, Victoria. *The Family Diagram and Family Research*. Houston: Center for the Study of Natural Systems and the Family, 2018.

Richardson, Ronald W. *Becoming a Healthier Pastor*. Minneapolis: Augsburg Fortress, 2005.

Smith, Kathleen. *Everything Isn't Terrible: Conquer Your Insecurities, Interrupt Your Anxiety, and Finally Calm Down*. New York: Balance, 2019.

Smith, Kathleen. *True to You: A Therapist's Guide to Stop Pleasing Others and Start Being Yourself*. New York: St. Martin's Essentials, 2024.

Software for Creating Genogram/Family Diagram

Genopro, http://www.genopro.com/.

Newsletters

Kathleen Smith, the Anxious Overachiever, https://theanxiousoverachiever.substack.com/.

Parker Palmer, Living the Questions, https://parkerjpalmer.substack.com/.

Podcasts/Apps

Bowen Family Systems Theory

Elevator Systems, https://livingsystems.ca/resources/elevator-systems-podcast
   -s1/.
The Leader's Journey, https://theleadersjourney.us/podcast/.

Prayer and Spirituality

On Being (with Krista Tippett), https://onbeing.org/.
Pray As You Go, https://prayasyougo.org/.

Family Systems Training Programs for Clergy

Bowen Center for the Study of the Family, Faith Leadership Programs, https://
   www.thebowencenter.org/faith-leadership-programs.
Center for Family Process (Bethesda, MD), https://www.centerforfamilyprocess
   .com/.
Columbia Seminary, https://www.ctsnet.edu/academics/lifelong-learning/
   pastoral-excellence-programs-courses/.
   - Leadership in Ministry (Atlanta, Montreat, NC, Richmond, VA, online).
   - Ministering to Ministers (for those who have experienced forced
     termination).
Healthy Congregations, https://www.healthycongregations.com/.
Leading with Depth (online), https://www.gentogenleadership.com/courses.
Lombard Mennonite Peace Center (Lombard, IL), https://www.lmpeacecenter
   .org/.

NOTES

Chapter 1

1 Julie Nolke, "I Don't Care," July 15, 2021. Accessed June 6, 2025. https://www
.youtube.com/watch?v=iO3Q-y1T1jM.

2 Ryan George, "The Guys Who Designed Teddy Bears," March 4, 2022.
Accessed June 6, 2025. https://www.youtube.com/watch?v=klnbe_VJI88&list
=PLRE-UFLEgWzCFru2DUUQoP_PzSjcKovP1&index=12.

3 Becky Chambers, *A Prayer for the Crown-Shy* (New York: Tom Doherty,
2022), 29. Recommended by Rev. Mindi Welton-Mitchell.

4 Patrick D. Miller, *The New Interpreter's Bible*, Vol. VI, ed. Leander Keck
(Nashville, TN: Abingdon Press, 2001), 627–8.

5 Jenny Blake, *Free Time* (London: Swift 2022), 130.

6 See Carmen Acevedo Butcher's outstanding new translation of Brother
Lawrence, *Practice of the Presence: A Revolutionary Translation*
(Minneapolis: Broadleaf Books, 2022).

7 M. Eugene Boring, *The New Interpreter's Bible*, Vol. VIII, ed. Leander Keck
(Nashville: Abingdon Press, 1995), 275.

8 Andy Raine and John T. Skinner, eds., *Celtic Daily Prayer* (London: Marshall
Pickering, 1994), 18 (Language updated).

Chapter 2

1 Dan Hotchkiss suggests developing an annual plan for ministry rather than
a big overarching mission. "How to Write a Vision Statement," August 20,
2018. Accessed June 6, 2025. https://www.congregationalconsulting.org/how
-to-write-a-vision-statement/.

2   Israel Galindo, "That Vision Thing," November 20, 2007. Accessed June 6, 2025. https://grace-ed.org/blog/archives/721.

3   For more on empowering lay leaders, see Israel Galindo, *The Hidden Lives of Congregations* (Herndon, Virginia: Alban, 2004), chapter 10, "The Focus of Congregational Leaders." An additional resource is Paul Stevens and Phil Collins, *The Equipping Pastor: A Systems Approach to Congregational Leadership* (Lanham, MD: Rowman & Littlefield, 1993).

4   Roberta Gilbert, *The Eight Concepts of Bowen Theory* (Falls Church and Basye, Virginia: Leading Systems Press, 2004), 6–9.

5   Kirk Byron Jones, "Are You Saying Your Prayers," interview by Margaret Marcuson, December 4, 2009.

6   Murray Bowen, *Family Therapy in Clinical Practice* (New York: Jason Aronson, 1978), 200–203.

7   Bowen, *Family Therapy*, 49.

Chapter 3

1   Bowen, *Family Therapy*, 373.

Chapter 4

1   I originally told this story in Margaret Marcuson, "Be the Least Anxious Person in the (Virtual) Room," *#InThisTogether*, ed. Curtis Ramsey-Lucas (Valley Forge: Judson Press, 2020), 47.

2   Personal communication.

3   Bowen, *Family Therapy*, 156.

4   Harriet Goldhor Lerner, *The Dance of Anger* (New York: Harper & Row, 1985) and *The Dance of Intimacy* (New York: Harper & Row, 1989).

5   One to try is Genopro, https://genopro.com/.

6 Israel Galindo et al., *A Family Genogram Workbook* (Educational Consultants, 2006).

7 Bowen, *Family Therapy*, 540.

8 Bowen, *Family Therapy*, 541.

9 *Family Therapy*, 542.

10 Martin Buber, *I and Thou*, trans. Walter Kaufmann (New York: Touchstone, 1971).

Chapter 5

1 *The New Yorker Book of Money Cartoons*, ed. Robert Mankoff (Princeton: Bloomberg Press, 1999), 35.

2 Peter Steinke, "How Do You Get Less Anxious about Church Finance?" interview by Margaret Marcuson, March 31, 2011.

3 Angelo Bolea, Lecture, Center for Family Process (Bethesda, MD, November 4, 1997).

4 Adapted from Edwin Friedman, *Generation to Generation* (New York: Guilford, 1985), 35–9.

5 I discuss this at length in "Remember Your Family's Money Story," *Money and Your Ministry* (Portland: Marcuson Leadership Circle, 2014), 70–88.

6 Personal interview, January 4, 2016. *Ministry and Money: A Practical Guide for Pastors*, by Janet T. Jamieson and Philip D. Jamieson (Louisville: Westminster John Knox, 2009), is a helpful resource book on church finance, including financial statements.

Chapter 6

1 Letter of November 23, 1964, *Commitment to Principles: The Letters of Murray Bowen, M.D.,* ed. Clarence Boyd (2008), 196. Electronic version available free at https://murraybowenarchives.org/boyd-book/.

2   Edwin Friedman, *A Failure of Nerve: Leadership in the Age of the Quick Fix*, ed. Margaret M. Treadwell and Edward W. Beal (New York: Seabury, 2007), 128.

3   Friedman, Lecture, Post Graduate Seminar in Family Emotional Process, Bethesda, MD, September 10, 1996. .

4   Friedman, *Failure*, 128.

5   Susan Scott, *Fierce Conversations: Achieving Success at Work & in Life, One Conversation at a Time* (New York: New American Library, 2017), 274.

6   Ronald W. Richardson, *Polarization and the Healthier Church* (2012) is an excellent resource for communicating in conflict, including listening.

7   *LogistiK,* August 28, 2013. Accessed June 7, 2025. https://www.youtube.com /watch?v=I47Y6VHc3Ms.

8   Warren, "An Open Letter to Southern Baptists," *Baptist News Global*, June 2, 2023. Accessed June 7, 2025. https://baptistnews.com/article/an-open-letter -to-all-southern-baptists/.

9   Bowen, *Family Therapy*, 252.

10 Katie Canales, "Tony Hsieh, the Late Former CEO of Zappos, Famously Pioneered the Concept of Paying New, Unhappy Employees $2,000 to Quit in Order to Maintain a Happy, Productive Workforce," *Business Insider,* November 30, 2020. Accessed June 7, 2025. https://www.businessinsider .com/zappos-tony-hsieh-paid-new-workers-to-quit-the-offer-2020-11?op =1.

11 Richardson, *Polarization*, 140.

12 See *Writing for Busy Readers: Communicate More Effectively in the Real World*, Todd Rogers and Jessica Lasky-Fink (New York: Dutton, 2023). Their website https://writingforbusyreaders.com/ offers an excellent resource for clearer written communication in emails and elsewhere.

Chapter 7

1   Anne Lamott, *Dusk, Night, Dawn: On Revival and Courage* (New York: Riverhead, 2021), 27.

2   Personal communication, May 5, 2025.

3   Two older books on Sabbath I've found helpful: Wayne Muller, *Sabbath: Finding Rest, Renewal, and Delight in Our Busy Lives* (New York: Random House, 2000) and Tilden Edwards, *Sabbath Time* (Nashville: Upper Room, 2003. Out of print, used copies available).

4   Noa Kagayama, "4 Signs You May Be Practicing Too Hard," *Bulletproof Musician,* February 16, 2012. Accessed June 7, 2025. https://bulletproofmusician.com/4-signs-you-may-be-practicing-too-hard/.

5   Check out this article from *Scientific American*: Ferris Jabr, "Why Your Brain Needs More Downtime," *Scientific American,* October 15, 2013. Accessed June 7, 2025. https://www.scientificamerican.com/article/mental-downtime/.

6   Kenneth Atchity, *Write Time: Guide to the Creative Process, from Vision through Revision—and Beyond* (Los Angeles: Story Merchant Books, 2014). Kindle edition, Loc 253.

7   Brett and Kate McKay, "On the Seventh Day, We Unplug: How and Why to Take a Tech Sabbath," *The Art of Manliness,* Last updated July 2, 2023. Accessed June 7, 2025. https://www.artofmanliness.com/character/advice/tech-sabbath/.

Chapter 8

1   Ed McManus, "The Jokesmith (1984–2012): The Last Issue," *The Jokesmith,* October 17, 2012. Accessed June 6, 2025. https://thejokesmith.wordpress.com/2012/10/17/the-jokesmith-1984-2012-the-last-issue/.

2   I focus on individual discernment here. Prayerful community discernment is also important. Two excellent resources for doing this work are: *How to Lead When You Don't Know Where You're Going: Leading in a Liminal Season,* by Susan Beaumont (Lanham, MD: Rowman & Littlefield, 2019) and *Grounded in God*, Suzanne G. Farnham, et al. (Harrisburg: Morehouse, 1999). See also the American nuns' response to a challenge from Vatican leadership for a wonderful case study of discernment through a time of crisis: *However Long the Night: Making Meaning in a Time of Crisis*, ed. Annmarie Sanders IHM (Silver Spring, MD: Leadership Conference of Women Religious, 2018).

3   Jones, "Are You Saying Your Prayers." See also his book *Rest in the Storm: Self-Care Strategies for Clergy and other Caregivers* (Valley Forge: Judson, 2021).

4   Angela Ashwin, *Woven Into Prayer* (Norwich: Canterbury, 1999), 204.

5   Margaret Treadwell, Presentation, Post Graduate Seminar in Family Emotional Process, Bethesda, MD, September 17, 1996.

6   Try an unstructured silent retreat, or one that follows the hours of prayer in a monastic retreat center. You might also try a silent retreat to reflect on your ministry and do some planning.

7   https://shalem.org/, and https://contemplativeoutreach.org/

8   His Holiness the Dalai Lama, "A Special Message from His Holiness the Dalai Lama," March 30, 2020. Accessed June 7, 2025. https://www.dalailama.com/news/2020/a-special-message-from-his-holiness-the-dalai-lama.

9   Personal communication, January 21, 2021.

10   John Chryssavgis, *In the Heart of the Desert* (Bloomington: World Wisdom, 2008), 98.

11   Martha Tatanic, "Getting Ultrareal About the Church," *Christiancentury.org,* August 2023. Accessed June 7, 2025. https://www.christiancentury.org/article/features/getting-ultrareal-about-church.

12   Margaret J. Wheatley, *So Far from Home: Lost and Found in Our Brave New World* (San Francisco: Berrett-Koehler, 2012), 10.

13   Treadwell, Presentation, Post Graduate Seminar in Family Emotional Process, 1996.

14   *The Oregonian*, August 22, 2002.

About the Author

Margaret J. Marcuson helps clergy get lighter and less burdened by their ministry so they can have more influence with less stress. She works with leaders from over 20 denominations across North America as teacher and coach. Margaret is the author of *Leaders Who Last* (2009) and *Money and Your Ministry* (2014). She has taught since 1999 in Leadership in Ministry, a family systems workshop for clergy. An American Baptist minister, she served as pastor at First Baptist Church, Gardner, Massachusetts, for 13 years. Margaret lives in Portland, Oregon, where she sings in two choirs. Find ministry resources at margaretmarcuson.com.